ASSERTING THE HUMAN DIGNITY: JUDGMENT OF THE SUPREME COURT OF INDIA ON TRANSGENDERS

By

Dr. Lokendra Malik

LL.M., Ph.D., LL.D. (N.L.S., Bangalore)
Advocate, Supreme Court of India, New Delhi

and

Ms. Anjum Hassan

B.A.LL.B., LL.M.
Assistant Professor of Law
I.M.S. Law College, NOIDA

Satyam Law International

ISBN: 978-93-82823-25-4

Published by : Satish Upadhyay, Satyam Law International 2/13, Ansari Road, Daryaganj, New Delhi-110 002, India

Phones   : 0091-11-23242686, 23245698

Fax   : 0091-11-23267131

Email   : customercare@satyambooks.net
                satyambooks@hotmail.com

Web   : www.satyambooks.net

Printed in India

Foreword by
Hon'ble Mr. Justice Deepak Verma,
former Judge, Supreme Court of India,
New Delhi

I am glad to learn that Dr. Lokendra Malik and Ms. Anjum Hassan are publishing a monograph titled. *"Asserting the Human Dignity: Judgment of the Supreme Court of India on Transgender"*. to be published by the Satyam Law International, New Delhi. This is indeed a great work that highlights the importance and relevance of the historic judgment of the Apex Court on transgenders.

In NALSA case. Supreme Court has done a highly commendable work. It is a historic step to abolish the gender based discrimination in the society. The judgment goes well with the letter and spirit of the constitutional democracy that provides same rights and constitutional protection to the transgenders as provided to all other citizens, that is, male and female. The verdict eliminates discrimination based on gender, especially gender as presumed to be assigned to individuals at birth and asserts their human dignity. It is a dignity cautious judgment. Further, beyond prohibiting discrimination and harassment of the transgenders. the Court has extended international principles of human dignity, freedom and autonomy to this unfairly marginalised and vulnerable section of the society which is the requirement of an inclusive healthy democracy based on rule of law and constitutionalism. The judgment propounds a comprehensive framework that takes into its fold not merely the negative right of the people against discrimination, but also "the positive right to make decisions about their lives, to express themselves and to choose which activities to take part in" which are deeply rooted in our constitutional scheme. In particular, direction of the Supreme Court that the transgender people should be treated as *'socially and educationally backward'* class of citizens and given reservation in educational institutions and government jobs is a far-reaching contribution to their all-round growth.

The Court has recently reiterated its stand in the case *of Ram Singh v. Union of India* to include the transgenders in the category of backward class of citizens. The jurisprudential foundation of the judgment is that sexual-identity cannot be based on a mere biological test but must take into account the individual's psyche or choice. The choice cannot be ignored. The Court has noted that Indian law treats gender as a binary male/female concept, with sections of the Indian Penal Code and Acts related to marriage, adoption, divorce, succession, and even welfare legislation, being examples. The Court has also relied on the Yogy akarta Principles — norms on sexual- orientation and gender-identity evolved in 2006 at Yogyakarta in Indonesia — to bolster its reasoning.

The judgment makes a good reading. The separate, but concurring, opinions of Justices K.S. Radhakrishnan and Dr. A.K. Sikri carry some healthy criticism of the earlier judgment in *Suresh Kumar Koushal* upholding Section 377 of Indian Penal Code that criminalises even consensual same-sex activity. While conscious that they cannot depart from the judgment of a Division Bench, both judges have highlighted the fact that misuse of Section 377 is one of the principal forms of discrimination against the transgender people. By noting that Section 377, despite being linked to some sexual acts, also highlights certain identities. Mr. Justice Radhakrishnan sees a link between gender-identity and sexual- orientation, something that the *Koushal* formulation missed, when it concluded that the provision criminalized the act and not any identity or orientation. The sentence that transgenders "even though insigniticant in numbers... have every right to enjoy their human rights" is a fitting rebuttal to the claim in *Koushal* that because the LGBT community is a minuscule minority, it could not be held that the section is invalid. Constitutional protection ought to be made available to a particular group regardless of its size. The verdict on the transgender community now provides one more reason why Section 377 ought to be amended to de-criminalize gay sex. Some international developments particularly judgment of the Supreme Court of the United States in same-sex marriage also dilutes the foundation of Koushal case and lays down the foundation stone of its overruling by a larger Bench in future.

The judgment of the Supreme on transgenders is historic one and the present monograph presents it beautifully along with its coverage by the national as well as international media. It has asserted the dignity of thousands of people who were denied their dues by the society for centuries and were fully left at the mercy of almighty. The judgment fulfills the visionary approach of the Founding Fathers and strengthens the constitutional ethos of equalitarian jurisprudence and fundamental rights regime. It invokes the conscience of the law-making authorities to legislate in the light of the judgment that has humanized the adjudication process.

I congratulate Dr. Lokendra Malik and Ms. Anjum Hassan to edit this monograph excellently. I hope the people would find it interesting and useful. Needless to say that both of them have done a commendable job and it highlights the salient features of the case in a vivid and in interesting manner. My heartiest congratulations to both for this excellent work.

New Delhi

Justice Deepak Verma (Retd.)

July 15, 2015

Preface

The judgment of the Supreme Court of India delivered in the case of *National Legal Services Authority v. Union of India*[1] on 15th April 2014 by a Division Bench comprising Justices K. S. Radhakrishnan and Dr. A. K. Sikri is a historical decision that will be a mile stone in the area of gender justice in the country and will have long term impact in the coming times to promote the equality jurisprudence. The verdict is a great example of recognition of right to life with dignity and is also an example of unique judicial craftsmanship and creativity on the part of the apex constitutional court of the country that decides the legal destiny of the nation by interpreting its Constitution and the statutes which ultimately makes all courts and tribunals bound to follow the its judgments as per the mandate of Article 141 of the Constitution. Though it was, and is, the duty of the Parliament to make a law on third gender and provide them necessary legal recognition for which they are fully entitled, it is only done by the Supreme Court in this judgment. The judgment is a constructive step towards the humanization of justice-delivery system in the country and has erased an injustice

---

[1] (2014) 5 SCC 438.

which was prevailing against lakhs of people for centuries in our society. The judgment conforms to the mandate of basic human rights and dignity of the people including third genders as enshrined in the fundamental law of the land drafted by eminent founding fathers such as Dr. B. R. Ambedkar, Pandit Jawaharlal Nehru, and Alladi Krishnaswamy Iyer and so on. It is another extended view of right to life under Article 21 of the Constitution and also an instance of asserting equality based legal order as enshrined under Article 14 of the Constitution. This judgment clearly reflects the judicial creativity of the Supreme Court.

The judgment in the NALSA case conforms the mandate of the international law and human rights conventions encouraging the law-makers of the country to incorporate the same into the municipal law of the land effectively which would be benefitting lakhs of people who were and still are humiliated for a long time and whose voice is not heard in the Parliament House or the State Legislative Assemblies as they do not have sufficient votes which could affect the results. Unfortunately in our country it is only the votes which count and not the voice. This judgment has brought the country into highest pedestrian of human rights jurisprudence giving meaning to the interpretation of right to life and human dignity enshrined under Article 21 of the Constitution. It is a unique example of equality jurisprudence inherent in Article 14 of the Constitution of India. The two great judges who pronounced this historic verdict deserve all appreciations and respect by all those who believe in a civilized legal order and inclusive growth jurisprudence based on humanized juristic philosophy. It promotes constitutional culture and morality in the country. "Constitutional morality is not a natural sentiment. It has to be cultivated. We must realize that our people have yet to learn it" said Dr. B.R. Ambedkar. This judgment fulfills the vision of Dr. Ambedkar and places India in the category of those civilized nations that focus on human development and growth in the best possible manner. The Court has touched all heights of human welfare in this judgment.

As mentioned earlier, the above mentioned judgment is a great example of judicial creativity. It proves that our judges not only adjudicate the legal issues but they enact the laws through their interpretation to do complete justice between the parties. It has been a matter of debate whether the judges make the law or just interpret it. In 1980, Lord Diplock said that "Parliament makes the laws, the judiciary interprets them".[2] By that he meant that, where Parliament has legislated, it is for the courts to interpret the legislation, not to rewrite it. But the statement is sometimes invoked to support the view that judges have no business in making law. That view fails to understand the nature of the task that a common law judge in developing the law. Judges are and always have been lawmakers; this is inherent in their constitutional role in a common law system which India has also followed. Indeed, even 150 years ago, and maybe more

---

[2] Duport Ltd v Sirs [1980] 1 WLR 142, 157 per Lord Diplock. See also Lord Mustill in Ex p Fire Bridges Union [1995] 2 AC 513 at 597.

[3] Jonathan Montgomery et al, Hidden Law-Making in the Province of Medical Jurisprudence (2014) 77(3) MLR 343.

recently, more English laws were made by judges than by legislators. The balance of the functions, a practical matter, may have changed, but the nature of the functions, a matter of fundamental principle, has not. The notion that Parliament is the only body engaged in law-making in the wider sense is demonstrably untrue and it does not involve so-called "judicial supremacism" to suggest otherwise. An article last year identified "tiers of relative invisibility' as the law-making function is diffused across a spectrum of "intermediate law-makers", such as lobbyists, regulatory bodies and Judges.[3] A judge is often called upon to make new law, whether by developing existing principles to address novel situations or lacunae, by interpreting and reinterpreting legislation and statutory instruments, or, more controversially, by revisiting established principles in light of social change. The NALSA verdict demonstrates this judicial creativity and craftsmanship of our Supreme Court.

Ever since the commencement of the Constitution the Supreme Court has been very active in protecting the fundamental rights of the people as enshrined in the Constitution and interpreted it in light of the international developments also. The Court always focused on rule of law and constitutionalism and protected people from excesses of officialdom. The Court made the law-making bodies more accountable and made some laws too. It is well-known how the Supreme Court put a brake on the amending power of the

---

[4] Golaknath v. State of Punjab, AIR 1967 SC 1643.
[5] Kesavananda Bharathi v. State of Kerala, AIR 1973 SC 1461.

Parliament in the *Golaknath case*.[4] Though after a few years the Supreme Court overruled the Golaknath judgment in the *Kesavananda Bharati*,[5] it imposed a heavy restriction on the Parliament in the latter case and held that the basic features of the Constitution cannot be altered or destroyed by the Parliament during the amendment process carried out as per Article 368 of the Constitution. The Public Interest Litigation jurisprudence has been created by the judiciary particularly the Supreme Court and is a clear example of judge-made law. The judgment in NALSA case is also an example of Public Interest Litigation jurisprudence which has enhanced the national prestige and dignity in the eyes of the international community.

It is a matter of fact that before this judgment there was no law to deal with the legal recognition of transgenders in the country and the Parliament left this matter at the mercy of god. It is a matter of deep concern that the law-makers in the land of Swami Vivekananda did not think it appropriate to spare some time on the problems of transgenders. The transgenders were not able to protect their dignity as they had been intended to indulge in begging and other mean jobs which were contrary to their dignity and the society treated them badly. They were not able to raise their voice through the electoral means as their voice was not heard by the law-makers but the apex court of the country heard their voice and came to their rescue. It is only the judgment delivered by two great Justices of the Supreme Court namely, Mr. Radhakrishnan and Dr. A. K. Sikri who asserted their rights and dignity through judicial process and compelled the arrogant and insensitive lawmakers to enact a law for their welfare and survival. Both great judges created a magna carta for thousands of transgenders in the country. After this judgment, a Bill has been passed by the Rajya Sabha and it is still waiting to be tabled in the Lok Sabha for necessary process. This judgment is a unique example of liberal interpretation of constitutional text in the light of humanitarian approach and democratic discourse. It humanizes the law. By this judgment began a new process of judicial assertiveness and the Court continued to engage in the law-making process through interpretation. This judgment is a great example of humanized judicial process.

The Constitution of India which is supreme law of the land provides fundamental rights to the people irrespective of their caste, class, and race, colour or gender in Part III against the State which is defined under Article 12 of the Constitution. In essence, the Constitution is 'sex blind'. It does not allow the lawmakers to discriminate on the basis of sex. Like the other people that is the ordinary male and female, the transgenders are also entitled to get the protection of fundamental rights such as equality before the law, and other rights as they constitute the corum of 'people of India'. Article 14 of the Constitution prohibits discrimination on the basis of sex. Other clauses of the article equally prohibit discrimination on the basis of sex if someone wants to have access to shops, public restaurants, hotels and places of public entertainment or the use of wells, tanks, bathing ghats,

---

[6] Article 32 of the Constitution of India.
[7] Article 226 of the Constitution of India.

roads and places of public resort maintained wholly or partly out of state funds or dedicated to the use of the general public. Similarly, Article 16 of the Constitution provides equality of opportunity in matters of public employment to all citizens under the state employment. And the state is prohibited to discriminate against any citizen on the basis of sex in giving public employment. Article 19 provides various freedoms to all citizens of India and Article 21 provides protection of life and personal liberty of any person. All these rights and freedoms are equally available to the transgenders also. But in practice the situation is entirely different. Whenever these people approach government functionaries for their rights, the government does not listen to them and takes the plea of gender binary. Consequently they are forced to indulge in inhumane acts which make them laughing stock in the eyes of the society. In fact, they are not at all considered as a part of society. They are deprived from the fruits of inclusive growth. The present judgment enforces all their fundamental rights.

The State, as defined under Article 12 of the Constitution, is mandated to honour the fundamental rights of the people and if it violates their fundamental rights, they can move to the Supreme Court[6] or the High Court[7] for getting relief. Not only against the State, but even against private persons some fundamental rights are enforceable like Article 17 and 23. Generally, as per Part III of the Constitution, the beneficiaries of the rights are identified as 'person' or 'citizen'. In the absence of any specific or implied exclusion or denial of such recognition, by virtue of the fact that a transgender is a human being, all fundamental rights must necessarily flow to a transgender also. The 'transgender' community falls within the purview of the Constitution of India and thereby they are fully entitled to all the rights as guaranteed under it. Unfortunately the term 'natural person' is interpreted as male and female of any age. The people who are neither male nor female are not included in the definition of person. This is a wrong practice as well as perception. Only the private part does not certify the identity of any human being. It is the physical persona and mental assets which matters. Except the private part, the God has given all faculties to the transgenders which they can exercise properly and make their visible contribution in the society if opportunities are given to them. The transgenders are citizens of India and are fully entitled to get the benefit of all schemes and programmes launched by the Government irrespective of their population. Now the Election Commission of India has also taken special measures to enroll the transgender persons as electors. The other lawmaking authorities should also take a lesson from the Election Commission and should recognize the third gender specifically in their documents. We have learnt that now the universities and colleges are also having a separate column in their admission forms for the transgenders.

This is a naked truth that lakhs of people are there who belong to this category of third gender and are deprived of the

---

[8] National Legal Services Authority of India v. Union of India, (2014) 5 SCC 438, at 442.

basic constitutional guarantees and other statutory protections. Without any fault on their part they have become the victims of grammatical interpretation by the state and humanity is thrown into dustbin by the lawmakers. Is it not against the human dignity? It is a gross violation of human rights and dignity as well as available under Article 21 of the Constitution. The police and municipal authorities treat these people badly and exploit them for many reasons which cannot be accepted in a constitutional democracy based on the rule of law. For many years, no affirmative action was taken by the Governments to recognize their gender and these people were thrown at the mercy of God who is the maker of the whole universe. It is only the Supreme Court that took the cognizance of their plights in the NALSA case and came to their rescue and recognized their dignity by declaring them third gender and directed the state to implement its verdict. This judgment humanized the law by giving protection to lakhs of people who were kept outside the citizenry for a long time by the law makers without any fault. As per the mandate of Article 141 of the Constitution the judgment has become the law of the land and the Government is bound to implement it in its letter and spirit under Article 144 of the Constitution. This judgment will be long remembered in the judicial history of India and the coming generations too will feel proud about it.

The NALSA verdict has protected the dignity of lakhs of people and gave them status and respect in the society that they

---

[9] Writ Petition(Civil) No. 274 of 2014, decided on 17 March 2015.

truly deserved. It gave them a confidence that they are also the part of the society like other males and females and have full stake in its welfare and have all rights to grow. They have all rights to get the benefit of fruits of an independent and secular country, a country which is based on the rule of law. It gave them a right to be the part of the electorate which elects its government periodically and also an opportunity to be the part of the lawmaking bodies. These people, who are born in the land of Mahatma, are very happy with this judgment of the apex court which has settled their fate. In fact, it is the path-finding judgment for them and their future generations. It gives them heavy relief from the trauma which they were facing for the centuries at the hands of the society, the society which treated them as untouchables. Neither education nor jobs were available to them and only begging had become their destiny. They were not allowed to be the part of public meetings and dialogues. They were treated uncivilized by so-called civilized men and women. In public places like railway stations, bus stands, schools, workplaces, malls, theatres, hospitals, everywhere they were sidelined and kept out of the social fabric. In his judgment in the NALSA case Justice Radhakrishnan admits this fact in these words: *"Seldom, our society realizes or cares to realize the trauma, agony and pain which the members of Transgender community neither undergo, nor appreciates the innate feelings of the members of the Transgender community, especially of those whose mind and body disown their biological sex. Our society often ridicules and abuses the Transgender community and in public places like railway stations, bus stands, schools, workplaces, malls, theatres, hospitals, they are sidelined and treated as untouchables, forgetting the fact that the moral failure lies in the society's unwillingness to contain or embrace different gender identities and expressions, a mindset which we have to change.*"[8] Indeed, these are shocking observations which need a serious consideration by the policy-makers and obligate them to legislate humanely.

It is submitted that by recognising the transgender community as a third gender entitled to the same rights and constitutional protection as all other citizens i.e. male and female, the Supreme Court has put in place a sound basis to end discrimination based on gender, especially gender as presumed to be assigned to individuals at birth. Further, beyond prohibiting discrimination and harassment, the Court has extended global principles of dignity, freedom and autonomy to this unfairly marginalised and vulnerable community and has met the norms of Universal Declaration of Human Rights. The judgment lays down a comprehensive framework that takes into its fold not merely the negative right against discrimination, but also "the positive right to make decisions about their lives, to express themselves and to choose which activities to take part in." It is not their birth duty to earn by begging or singing and dancing on roads. They are equally entitled to be the part of the public services and other jobs. In particular, the direction of the court that they should be treated as 'socially and educationally backward' and given reservation in education and employment, is a far-reaching contribution to their all-round development. Recently the Supreme Court has reiterated its stand for including the transgenders in the category of other backward classes in *Ram Singh v. Union of India*[9] case. Appreciating the NALSA case the Supreme Court observed in this case:

> The recognition of the third gender as a socially and educationally backward class of citizens entitled to affirmative action of the State under the Constitution in National Legal Services Authority vs. Union of India is too significant a development to be ignored. In fact it is a path finder, if not a path-breaker. It is an important reminder to the State of the high degree of vigilance it must exercise to discover emerging forms of backwardness. The State, therefore, cannot blind itself to the existence of other forms and instances of backwardness. An affirmative action policy that keeps in mind only historical injustice would certainly result in under-protection of the most deserving backward class of citizens, which is constitutionally mandated. It is the identification of these new emerging groups that must engage the attention of the State and the constitutional power and duty must be concentrated to discover such groups rather than to enable groups of citizens to recover "lost ground' in claiming preference and benefits on the basis of historical prejudice.

The abovementioned observations compel the government to take a note of third gender in the society. It reiterates the previous observations given in the NALSA case. The jurisprudential basis for the judgment in the NALSA case is that sex identity cannot be based on a mere biological test but must take into account the individual's psyche. The Court has noted that Indian law treats gender as a binary male/female concept, with sections of the Indian Penal Code and Acts related to marriage, adoption, divorce, succession, and even welfare legislation, being examples. The Court has also relied on the Yogyakarta Principles — norms on sexual orientation and gender identity evolved in 2006 at Yogyakarta in Indonesia — to bolster its reasoning. But only the judicial verdict is not sufficient. There is an urgent need of attitudinal change in the society. The society would have to accept these people so that they should not feel segregated. The society should bring these people in mainstream. The Supreme Court has given the society a chance to contribute for these people so that we might achieve our common goal of inclusive growth and equalitarian development.

The NALSA case will give huge relief to the transgenders who were persecuted for centuries by the society. By virtue of this judgment, all identity documents, including a birth certificate, passport, ration card and driving license would recognise the third gender. It is a historical judgment. It has determined the legal destiny of lakhs of people whose human rights were willfully violated by the state for a long time. The Supreme Court has declared the law in favour of these people who have become the part of *"We, the People of India"*, the people who made their supreme law of the land. It will certainly please our Founding Fathers who are sitting in the heaven that their people are happy and prosperous and the document which they drafted to govern the nation is governing the nation well. It will make the legal order human friendly and inclusive and international law friendly. The judgment is a great example of humanitarian adjudication.

Now as the transgenders are recognized as third gender in the legal documents by all states and their agencies, the third gender people can move to courts of law if any of their right is violated by the state or even private persons also as access to justice is the essence of rule of law. The hammer of Article 144 of the Constitution will compel the state and its instrumentalities to implement the verdict of the Supreme Court in its letter and spirit. Let us hope that the Government implements the verdict of the Supreme Court honestly and gives these people their dues for which they are fully entitled. It is a matter of fact that though this judgment is a historical judgment which has protected the dignity and identity of the transgender, only this verdict is not sufficient. This verdict should be implemented by the Central Government, State Governments, and all other agencies of the Government in toto and a particular policy should be framed by the different ministries/departments to prepare a national plan for the welfare of transgenders. The Government should constitute a National Commission for the Transgenders which should look after the interests of these people and protect their rights effectively. If possible, either the constitutional or statutory status should be given to this commission. Until and unless the transgenders get a fair deal, the vision of inclusive growth set by the founding fathers can never be achieved in this land of Buddha. This is not only the duty of the state but it is a collective duty of all of us which we must discharge truly and sincerely.

It is a matter of deep concern that despite the submission of the report by an expert committee to the Ministry of Social Justice and Empowerment, Government of India, the recommendations of the committee are yet to be implemented by the Centre and the States. It shows that the Governments are not taking the welfare of transgenders seriously as they do not constitute a visible electoral constituency. This matter needs a serious consideration and the Government should take it seriously and frame the national policy for these people as soon as possible.

The present monograph presents the historical judgment of the Supreme Court along with its appreciation by the international media. Its main purpose is to widely circulate the judgment among the scholars and intellectuals from inter-disciplinary approach so that a national debate could take place pertaining to the legal rights and duties of the transgenders in the society and an attitudinal change could be achieved. Until and unless the society changes its attitude towards the transgenders no efforts taken by the government or the judiciary can be successful. We hope that it would generate a new debate among the scholars for welfare of the transgenders and will certainly strengthen the judicial verdict.

We declare that we have included the coverage of different national as well as international dailies in the present volume and we duly acknowledge it in our work. Following works are fully acknowledged by us with sincere thanks to republish them in our volume:

1. Chapal Mehra, Ending the gender binary, The Hindu, 22 April, 2014.

2. Editorial Board, The New York Times, Transgender Rights in India, The New York Times, 25 April, 2014.

3. Editorial, The Hindu, Salutary Judgment, The Hindu, 17 April, 2014.

4. Ratna Kapur, Beyond Male and Female, The Right to Humanity, The Hindu, 19 April, 2014.

5. Homa Khaleeli, Hijra: India's Third Gender Claims its place in Law, The Guardian, 16 April, 2014.

6. Ash Kotak, India's Transgender Law is no help to its lesbian, gay and bisexual communities, The Guardian, 17 April, 2014

7. Sophie McBain, India's Supreme Court recognises a Third Gender, New Statesman, 16 April, 2014.

8. Nikita Lalwani, India's Supreme Court: Transgender is a Third Legal Gender The Wall Street Journal, April 15, 2014.

9. Adam Withnall, India court recognises transgender people as 'third gender' The Independent, April 16, 2014.

10. Dean Nelson, India's Supreme Court creates official

third sex for eunuchs and transgenders, The Telegraph, 15 April 2014.

11. Harish V. Nair, Supreme Court recognises Transgender people as a "Third Gender" as it calls for an end to discrimination, Mail Online India, 15 April 2014.

12. Terrence McCoy, India now recognizes transgender citizens as 'third gender' The Washington Post, April 15, 2014

The contributions of the above mentioned persons have enhanced the academic beauty as well as value of our volume. We are highly grateful to Hon'ble Mr. Justice Deepak Verma, former Judge, Supreme Court of India for writing an erudite Foreword for our book. We are publishing it in public interest to sensitize the people to change their attitude towards transgender people so that an inclusive society could be made in the country. We sincerely hope that the work which we have undertaken would strengthen the debate on third gender in the country and would encourage the policy-makers to make better provisions for the transgenders in the country. We thank the publishers for publishing this monograph with high quality.

Dr. Lokendra Malik and Ms. Anjum Hassan

New Delhi

9 July, 2015

Contents

Foreword iii

Preface vii

PART **A**

[1-112]

Judgment of the Supreme Court of India in NALSA Case

PART **B**

[113-150]

Appreciation of the Judgment by National as well as International Media

1. Ending the Gender Binary 115

2. Transgender Rights in India 119

3. Salutary Judgment 121

4. Beyond Male and Female, the Right to
    Humanity 123

5. Hijra: India's Third Gender Claims its Place
    in Law 127

6. India's Transgender Law is no Help to its Lesbian,
    Gay and Bisexual Communities 130

7. India's Supreme Court Recognises a Third Gender 133

8. India's Supreme Court: Transgender is a Third Legal Gender 136

9. India Court Recognises Transgender People as 'Third Gender' 139

10. India's Supreme Court Creates Official Third Sex for Eunuchs and Transgenders 142

11. Supreme Court Recognises Transgender People as a "Third Gender" as it Calls for an End to Discrimination 145

12. India Now Recognizes Transgender Citizens as 'Third Gender' 148

PART **A**

Judgment of the Supreme Court of India in NALSA Case

NATIONAL LEGAL SERVICES AUTHORITY... Petitioner

Versus

UNION OF INDIA AND OTHERS... Respondents

Writ Petition (Civil) No. 400 of 2012, with No. 604 of 2013, decided on April 15, 2014

Before K. S. P. Radhakrishnan and Dr. A. K. Sikri, JJ.

K.S. Radhakrishnan, J. (Sikri, J. concurring)

1. Seldom, our society realizes or cares to realize the trauma, agony and pain which the members of Transgender community undergo, nor appreciates the innate feelings of the members of the Transgender community, especially of those whose mind and body disown their biological sex. Our society often ridicules and abuses the Transgender community and in public places like railway stations, bus stands, schools, workplaces, malls, theatres, hospitals, they are sidelined and treated as untouchables, forgetting the fact that the moral failure lies in the society's unwillingness to contain or embrace different gender identities and expressions, a mindset which we have to change.

2. We are, in this case, concerned with the grievances of the members of Transgender Community (for short 'TG community') who seek a legal declaration of their gender identity than the one assigned to them, male or female,

at the time of birth and their prayer is that non-recognition of their gender identity violates Articles 14 and 21 of the Constitution of India. Hijras/Eunuchs, who also fall in that group, claim legal status as a third gender with all legal and constitutional protection.

3. The National Legal Services Authority, constituted under the Legal Services Authority Act, 1997, to provide free legal services to the weaker and other marginalized sections of the society, has come forward to advocate their cause, by filing Writ Petition No. 400 of 2012. Poojaya Mata Nasib Kaur Ji Women Welfare Society, a registered association, has also preferred Writ Petition No. 604 of 2013, seeking similar reliefs in respect of Kinnar community, a TG community.

4. Laxmi Narayan Tripathy, claimed to be a Hijra, has also got impleaded so as to effectively put across the cause of the members of the transgender community and Tripathy's life experiences also for recognition of their identity as a third gender, over and above male and female. Tripathy says that non-recognition of the identity of Hijras, a TG community, as a third gender, denies them the right of equality before the law and equal protection of law guaranteed under Article 14 of the Constitution and violates the rights guaranteed to them under Article 21 of the Constitution of India.

5. Shri Raju Ramachandran, learned senior counsel appearing for the petitioner – the National Legal Services

Authority, highlighted the traumatic experiences faced by the members of the TG community and submitted that every person of that community has a legal right to decide their sex orientation and to espouse and determine their identity. Learned senior counsel has submitted that since the TGs are neither treated as male or female, nor given the status of a third gender, they are being deprived of many of the rights and privileges which other persons enjoy as citizens of this country. TGs are deprived of social and cultural participation and hence restricted access to education, health care and public places which deprives them of the Constitutional guarantee of equality before law and equal protection of laws. Further, it was also pointed out that the community also faces discrimination to contest election, right to vote, employment, to get licences etc. and, in effect, treated as an outcast and untouchable. Learned senior counsel also submitted that the State cannot discriminate them on the ground of gender, violating Articles 14 to 16 and 21 of the Constitution of India.

6. Shri Anand Grover, learned senior counsel appearing for the Intervener, traced the historical background of the third gender identity in India and the position accorded to them in the Hindu Mythology, Vedic and Puranic literatures, and the prominent role played by them in the royal courts of the Islamic world etc. Reference was also made to the repealed Criminal Tribes Act, 1871 and

explained the inhuman manner by which they were treated at the time of the British Colonial rule. Learned senior counsel also submitted that various International Forums and U.N. Bodies have recognized their gender identity and referred to the Yogyakarta Principles and pointed out that those principles have been recognized by various countries around the world. Reference was also made to few legislations giving recognition to the trans-sexual persons in other countries. Learned senior counsel also submitted that non-recognition of gender identity of the transgender community violates the fundamental rights guaranteed to them, who are citizens of this country.

7. Shri T. Srinivasa Murthy, learned counsel appearing in I.A. No. 2 of 2013, submitted that transgender persons have to be declared as a socially and educationally backward classes of citizens and must be accorded all benefits available to that class of persons, which are being extended to male and female genders. Learned counsel also submitted that the right to choose one's gender identity is integral to the right to lead a life with dignity, which is undoubtedly guaranteed by Article 21 of the Constitution of India. Learned counsel, therefore, submitted that, subject to such rules/regulations/ protocols, transgender persons may be afforded the right of choice to determine whether to opt for male, female or transgender classification.

8. Shri Sanjeev Bhatnagar, learned counsel appearing for the petitioner in Writ Petition No.604 of 2013, highlighted the cause of the Kinnar community and submitted that they are the most deprived group of transgenders and calls for constitutional as well as legal protection for their identity and for other socio-economic benefits, which are otherwise extended to the members of the male and female genders in the community.

9. Shri Rakesh K. Khanna, learned Additional Solicitor General, appearing for the Union of India, submitted that the problems highlighted by the transgender community is a sensitive human issue, which calls for serious attention. Learned ASG pointed out that, under the aegis of the Ministry of Social Justice and Empowerment (for short "MOSJE"), a Committee, called "Expert Committee on Issues relating to Transgender", has been constituted to conduct an in-depth study of the problems relating to transgender persons to make appropriate recommendations to MOSJE. Shri Khanna also submitted that due representation would also be given to the applicants, appeared before this Court in the Committee, so that their views also could be heard.

10. We also heard learned counsel appearing for various States and Union Territories who have explained the steps they have taken to improve the conditions and

status of the members of TG community in their respective States and Union Territories.

11. Laxmi Narayan Tripathy, a Hijra, through a petition supported by an affidavit, highlighted the trauma undergone by Tripathy from Tripathy's birth. Rather than explaining the same by us, it would be appropriate to quote in Tripathy's own words:

"That the Applicant has born as a male. Growing up as a child, she felt different from the boys of her age and was feminine in her ways. On account of her femininity, from an early age, she faced repeated sexual harassment, molestation and sexual abuse, both within and outside the family. Due to her being different, she was isolated and had no one to talk to or express her feelings while she was coming to terms with her identity. She was constantly abused by everyone as a 'chakka' and 'hijra'. Though she felt that there was no place for her in society, she did not succumb to the prejudice. She started to dress and appear in public in women's clothing in her late teens but she did not identify as a woman. Later, she joined the Hijra community in Mumbai as she identified with the other hijras and for the first time in her life, she felt at home.

That being a hijra, the Applicant has faced serious discrimination throughout her life because of her gender identity. It has been clear to the Applicant that the complete non-recognition of the identity of hijras/transgender persons by the State has resulted in the violation of most of the fundamental rights guaranteed to them under the Constitution of India...."

12. Siddarth Narrain, eunuch, highlights Narrain's feeling, as follows:

"Ever since I can remember, I have always identified myself as a woman. I lived in Namakkal, a small town in Tamil Nadu. When I was in the 10th standard I realized that the only way for me to be comfortable was to join the hijra community. It was then that my family found out that I frequently met hijras who lived in the city. One day, when my father was away, my brother, encouraged by my mother, started beating me with a cricket bat. I locked myself in a room to escape from the beatings. My mother and brother then tried to break into the room to beat me up further. Some of my relatives intervened and brought me out of the room. I related my ordeal to an uncle of mine who gave me Rs.50 and asked me to go home. Instead, I took the money and went to live with a group of hijras in Erode."

Sachin, a TG, expressed his experiences as follows:

"My name is Sachin and I am 23 years old. As a child I always enjoyed putting make-up like 'vibhuti' or 'kum kum' and my parents always saw me as a girl. I am male but I only have female feelings. I used to help my mother in all the housework like cooking, washing and cleaning. Over the years, I started assuming more of the domestic responsibilities at home. The neighbours starting teasing me. They would call out to me and ask: 'Why don't you go out and work like a man?' or 'Why are you staying at home like a girl?' But I liked being a girl. I felt shy about going out and working. Relatives would also mock and scold me on this score. Every day I would go out of the house to bring water. And as I walked back with the water I would always be teased. I felt very ashamed. I even felt suicidal. How could I live like that? But my parents never protested. They were helpless."

We have been told and informed of similar life experiences faced by various others who belong to the TG community.

13. Transgender is generally described as an umbrella term for persons whose gender identity, gender expression or behavior does not conform to their biological sex. TG may also takes in persons who do not identify with their sex assigned at birth, which include Hijras/Eunuchs who, in this writ petition, describe themselves as "third gender" and they do not identify as either male or female. Hijras are not men by virtue of anatomy

appearance and psychologically, they are also not women, though they are like women with no female reproduction organ and no menstruation. Since Hijras do not have reproduction capacities as either men or women, they are neither men nor women and claim to be an institutional "third gender". Among Hijras, there are emasculated (castrated, nirvana) men, non-emasculated men (not castrated/akva/akka) and inter-sexed persons (hermaphrodites). TG also includes persons who intend to undergo Sex Re Assignment Surgery (SRS) or have undergone SRS to align their biological sex with their gender identity in order to become male or female. They are generally called transsexual persons. Further, there are persons who like to cross-dress in clothing of opposite gender, i.e. transvestites. Resultantly, the term "transgender", in contemporary usage, has become an umbrella term that is used to describe a wide range of identities and experiences, including but not limited to pre-operative, post-operative and non-operative transsexual people, who strongly identify with the gender opposite to their biological sex; male and female.

Historical Background of Transgenders in India

14. TG Community comprises of Hijras, eunuchs, Kothis, Aravanis, Jogappas, Shiv-Shakthis etc. and they, as a group, have got a strong historical presence in our country in the Hindu mythology and other religious

texts. The Concept of tritiya prakrti or napunsaka has also been an integral part of vedic and puranic literatures. The word 'napunsaka' has been used to denote absence of procreative capability.

15. Lord Rama, in the epic Ramayana, was leaving for the forest upon being banished from the kingdom for 14 years, turns around to his followers and asks all the 'men and women' to return to the city. Among his followers, the hijras alone do not feel bound by this direction and decide to stay with him. Impressed with their devotion, Rama sanctions them the power to confer blessings on 11 people on auspicious occasions like childbirth and marriage, and also at inaugural functions which, it is believed set the stage for the custom of badhai in which hijras sing, dance and confer blessings.

16. Aravan, the son of Arjuna and Nagakanya in Mahabharata, offers to be sacrificed to Goddess Kali to ensure the victory of the Pandavas in the Kurukshetra war, the only condition that he made was to spend the last night of his life in matrimony. Since no woman was willing to marry one who was doomed to be killed, Krishna assumes the form of a beautiful woman called Mohini and marries him. The Hijras of Tamil Nadu consider Aravan their progenitor and call themselves Aravanis.

17. Jain Texts also make a detailed reference to TG which mentions the concept of 'psychological sex'. Hijras also

played a prominent role in the royal courts of the Islamic world, especially in the Ottaman empires and the Mughal rule in the Medieval India. A detailed analysis of the historical background of the same finds a place in the book of Gayatri Reddy, "With Respect to Sex: Negotiating Hijra Identity in South India" – Yoda Press (2006).

18. We notice that even though historically, Hijras/ transgender persons had played a prominent role, with the onset of colonial rule from the 18th century onwards, the situation had changed drastically. During the British rule, a legislation was enacted to supervise the deeds of Hijras/TG community, called the Criminal Tribes Act, 1871, which deemed the entire community of Hijras persons as innately 'criminal' and 'addicted to the systematic commission of non-bailable offences'. The Act provided for the registration, surveillance and control of certain criminal tribes and eunuchs and had penalized eunuchs, who were registered, and appeared to be dressed or ornamented like a woman, in a public street or place, as well as those who danced or played music in a public place. Such persons also could be arrested without warrant and sentenced to imprisonment up to two years or fine or both. Under the Act, the local government had to register the names and residence of all eunuchs residing in that area as well as of their properties, who were reasonably suspected of kidnapping or castrating

children, or of committing offences under Section 377 of the IPC, or of abetting the commission of any of the said offences. Under the Act, the act of keeping a boy under 16 years in the charge of a registered eunuch was made an offence punishable with imprisonment up to two years or fine and the Act also denuded the registered eunuchs of their civil rights by prohibiting them from acting as guardians to minors, from making a gift deed or a will, or from adopting a son. Act has, however, been repealed in August 1949.

19. Section 377 of the IPC found a place in the Indian Penal Code, 1860, prior to the enactment of Criminal Tribles Act that criminalized all penile-non-vaginal sexual acts between persons, including anal sex and oral sex, at a time when transgender persons were also typically associated with the prescribed sexual practices. Reference may be made to the judgment of the Allahabad High Court in Queen Empress v. Khairati (1884) ILR 6 All 204, wherein a transgender person was arrested and prosecuted under Section 377 on the suspicion that he was a 'habitual sodomite' and was later acquitted on appeal. In that case, while acquitting him, the Sessions Judge stated as follows:

"This case relates to a person named Khairati, over whom the police seem to have exercised some sort of supervision, whether strictly regular or not, as a eunuch. The man is not a eunuch in the literal sense, but he was called for by the police when on a visit to his village, and was found singing dressed as a woman among the women of a certain family. Having been subjected to examination by the Civil Surgeon (and a subordinate medical man), he is shown to have the characteristic mark of a habitual catamite – the distortion of the orifice of the anus into the shape of a trumpet and also to be affected with syphilis in the same region in a manner which distinctly points to unnatural intercourse within the last few months."

Even though, he was acquitted on appeal, this case would demonstrate that Section 377, though associated with specific sexual acts, highlighted certain identities, including Hijras and was used as an instrument of harassment and physical abuse against Hijras and transgender persons.

20. A Division Bench of this Court in *Suresh Kumar Koushal and another v. Naz Foundation and others* [(2014) 1 SCC 1] has already spoken on the constitutionality of Section 377 IPC and, hence, we express no opinion on it since we are in these cases concerned with an altogether different issue pertaining to the constitutional and other legal rights of the transgender community and their gender identity and sexual orientation.

GENDER IDENTITY AND SEXUAL ORIENTATION

21. Gender identity is one of the most-fundamental aspects of life which refers to a person's intrinsic sense of being male, female or transgender or transsexual person. A person's sex is usually assigned at birth, but a relatively small group of persons may born with bodies which incorporate both or certain aspects of both male and female physiology. At times, genital anatomy problems may arise in certain persons, their innate perception of themselves, is not in conformity with the sex assigned to them at birth and may include pre and post-operative transsexual persons and also persons who do not choose to undergo or do not have access to operation and also include persons who cannot undergo successful operation. Countries, all over the world, including India, are grappled with the question of attribution of gender to persons who believe that they belong to the opposite sex. Few persons undertake surgical and other procedures to alter their bodies and physical appearance to acquire gender characteristics of the sex which conform to their perception of gender, leading to legal and social complications since official record of their gender at birth is found to be at variance with the assumed gender identity. Gender identity refers to each person's deeply felt internal and individual experience of gender, which may or may not correspond with the sex assigned at birth, including the personal sense of the body which

may involve a freely chosen, modification of bodily appearance or functions by medical, surgical or other means and other expressions of gender, including dress, speech and mannerisms. Gender identity, therefore, refers to an individual's self-identification as a man, woman, transgender or other identified category.

22. Sexual orientation refers to an individual's enduring physical, romantic and/or emotional attraction to another person. Sexual orientation includes transgender and gender-variant people with heavy sexual orientation and their sexual orientation may or may not change during or after gender transmission, which also includes homo-sexuals, bysexuals, heterosexuals, asexual etc. Gender identity and sexual orientation, as already indicated, are different concepts. Each person's self-defined sexual orientation and gender identity is integral to their personality and is one of the most basic aspects of self-determination, dignity and freedom and no one shall be forced to undergo medical procedures, including SRS, sterilization or hormonal therapy, as a requirement for legal recognition of their gender identity.

UNITED NATIONS AND OTHER HUMAN RIGHTS BODIES – ON GENDER IDENTITY AND SEXUAL ORIENTATION

23. United Nations has been instrumental in advocating the protection and promotion of rights of sexual minorities, including transgender persons. Article 6 of the Universal

Declaration of Human Rights, 1948 and Article 16 of the International Covenant on Civil and Political Rights, 1966 (ICCPR) recognize that every human being has the inherent right to live and this right shall be protected by law and that no one shall be arbitrarily denied of that right. Everyone shall have a right to recognition, everywhere as a person before the law. Article 17 of the ICCPR states that no one shall be subjected to arbitrary or unlawful interference with his privacy, family, home or correspondence, nor to unlawful attacks on his honour and reputation and that everyone has the right to protection of law against such interference or attacks. International Commission of Jurists and the International Service for Human Rights on behalf of a coalition of human rights organizations, took a project to develop a set of international legal principles on the application of international law to human rights violations based on sexual orientation and sexual identity to bring greater clarity and coherence to State's human rights obligations.

24. A distinguished group of human rights experts has drafted, developed, discussed and reformed the principles in a meeting held at Gadjah Mada University in Yogyakarta, Indonesia from 6 to 9 November, 2006, which is unanimously adopted the Yogyakarta Principles on the application of International Human Rights Law in relation to Sexual Orientation and Gender Identity.

Yogyakarta Principles address a broad range of human rights standards and their application to issues of sexual orientation gender identity. Reference to few Yogyakarta Principles would be useful.

YOGYAKARTA PRINCIPLES:

25. Principle 1 which deals with the right to the universal enjoyment of human rights, reads as follows :

1. The right to the universal enjoyment of human rights

All human beings are born free and equal in dignity and rights. Human beings of all sexual orientations and gender identities are entitled to the full enjoyment of all human rights.

States shall:

A. Embody the principles of the universality, interrelatedness, interdependence and indivisibility of all human rights in their national constitutions or other appropriate legislation and ensure the practical realisation of the universal enjoyment of all human rights;

B. Amend any legislation, including criminal law, to ensure its consistency with the universal enjoyment of all human rights;

C. Undertake programmes of education and awareness to promote and enhance the full enjoyment of all human rights by all persons, irrespective of sexual orientation or gender identity;

D. Integrate within State policy and decision-making a pluralistic approach that recognises and affirms the interrelatedness and indivisibility of all aspects of human identity including sexual orientation and gender identity.

2. The rights to equality and nondiscrimination

Everyone is entitled to enjoy all human rights without discrimination on the basis of sexual orientation or gender identity. Everyone is entitled to equality before the law and the equal protection of the law without any such discrimination whether or not the enjoyment of another human right is also affected. The law shall prohibit any such discrimination and guarantee to all persons equal and effective protection against any such discrimination. Discrimination on the basis of sexual orientation or gender identity includes any distinction, exclusion, restriction or preference based on sexual orientation or gender identity which has the purpose or effect of nullifying or impairing equality before the law or the equal protection of the law, or the recognition, enjoyment or exercise, on an equal basis, of all human rights and fundamental freedoms. Discrimination based on sexual orientation or gender identity may be, and commonly is, compounded by discrimination on other grounds including gender, race, age, religion, disability, health and economic status.

States shall:

A. Embody the principles of equality and nondiscrimination on the basis of sexual orientation and gender identity in their national constitutions or other appropriate legislation, if not yet incorporated therein, including by means of amendment and interpretation, and ensure the effective realisation of these principles;

B. Repeal criminal and other legal provisions that prohibit or are, in effect, employed to prohibit consensual sexual activity among people of the same sex who are over the age of consent, and ensure that an equal age of consent applies to both same-sex and different- sex sexual activity;

C. Adopt appropriate legislative and other measures to prohibit and eliminate discrimination in the public and private spheres on the basis of sexual orientation and gender identity;

D. Take appropriate measures to secure adequate advancement of persons of diverse sexual orientations and gender identities as may be necessary to ensure such groups or individuals equal enjoyment or exercise of human rights. Such measures shall not be deemed to be discriminatory;

E. In all their responses to discrimination on the basis of sexual orientation or gender identity, take account of the manner in which such discrimination may intersect with other forms of discrimination;

F. Take all appropriate action, including programmes of education and training, with a view to achieving the elimination of prejudicial or discriminatory attitudes or behaviours which are related to the idea of the inferiority or the superiority of any sexual orientation or gender identity or gender expression.

3. The right to recognition before the law

Everyone has the right to recognition everywhere as a person before the law. Persons of diverse sexual orientations and gender identities shall enjoy legal capacity in all aspects of life. Each person's self-defined sexual orientation and gender identity is integral to their personality and is one of the most basic aspects of self-determination, dignity and freedom. No one shall be forced to undergo medical procedures, including sex reassignment surgery, sterilisation or hormonal therapy, as a requirement for legal recognition of their gender identity. No status, such as marriage or parenthood, may be invoked as such to prevent the legal recognition of a person's gender identity. No one shall be subjected to pressure to conceal, suppress or deny their sexual orientation or gender identity.

States shall:

A. Ensure that all persons are accorded legal capacity in civil matters, without discrimination on the basis of sexual orientation or gender identity, and the opportunity to exercise that capacity, including equal rights to conclude contracts, and to administer, own, acquire (including through inheritance), manage, enjoy and dispose of property;

B. Take all necessary legislative, administrative and other measures to fully respect and legally recognise each person's self-defined gender identity;

C. Take all necessary legislative, administrative and other measures to ensure that procedures exist whereby all State-issued identity papers which indicate a person's gender/sex — including birth certificates, passports, electoral records and other documents — reflect the person's profound selfdefined gender identity;

D. Ensure that such procedures are efficient, fair and non-discriminatory, and respect the dignity and privacy of the person concerned;

E. Ensure that changes to identity documents will be recognised in all contexts where the identification or disaggregation of persons by gender is required by law or policy;

F. Undertake targeted programmes to provide social

support for all persons experiencing gender transitioning or reassignment.

4. The right to life

Everyone has the right to life. No one shall be arbitrarily deprived of life, including by reference to considerations of sexual orientation or gender identity. The death penalty shall not be imposed on any person on the basis of consensual sexual activity among persons who are over the age of consent or on the basis of sexual orientation or gender identity.

States shall:

A. Repeal all forms of crime that have the purpose or effect of prohibiting consensual sexual activity among persons of the same sex who are over the age of consent and, until such provisions are repealed, never impose the death penalty on any person convicted under them;

B. Remit sentences of death and release all those currently awaiting execution for crimes relating to consensual sexual activity among persons who are over the age of consent;

C. Cease any State-sponsored or State-condoned attacks on the lives of persons based on sexual orientation or gender identity, and ensure that all such attacks, whether by government officials or by any individual or group, are vigorously investigated, and that, where appropriate evidence is found, those responsible are prosecuted, tried and duly punished.

6. The right to privacy

Everyone, regardless of sexual orientation or gender identity, is entitled to the enjoyment of privacy without arbitrary or unlawful interference, including with regard to their family, home or correspondence as well as to protection from unlawful attacks on their honour and reputation. The right to privacy ordinarily includes the choice to disclose or not to disclose information relating to one's sexual orientation or gender identity, as well as decisions and choices regarding both one's own body and consensual sexual and other relations with others.

States shall:

A. Take all necessary legislative, administrative and other measures to ensure the right of each person, regardless of sexual orientation or gender identity, to enjoy the private sphere, intimate decisions, and human relations, including consensual sexual activity among persons who are over the age of consent, without arbitrary interference;

B. Repeal all laws that criminalise consensual sexual activity among persons of the same sex who are over the age of consent, and ensure that an equal age of consent applies to both same-sex and different-sex sexual activity;

C. Ensure that criminal and other legal provisions of general application are not applied to de facto criminalise consensual sexual activity among persons of the same sex who are over the age of consent;

D. Repeal any law that prohibits or criminalises the expression of gender identity, including through dress, speech or mannerisms, or that denies to individuals the opportunity to change their bodies as a means of expressing their gender identity;

E. Release all those held on remand or on the basis of a criminal conviction, if their detention is related to consensual sexual activity among persons who are over the age of consent, or is related to gender identity;

F. Ensure the right of all persons ordinarily to choose when, to whom and how to disclose information pertaining to their sexual orientation or gender identity, and protect all persons from arbitrary or unwanted disclosure, or threat of disclosure of such information by others.

9. The right to treatment with humanity while in detention

Everyone deprived of liberty shall be treated with humanity and with respect for the inherent dignity of the human person. Sexual orientation and gender identity are integral to each person's dignity.

States shall:

A. Ensure that placement in detention avoids further marginalising persons on the basis of sexual orientation or gender identity or subjecting them to risk of violence, ill-treatment or physical, mental or sexual abuse;

B. Provide adequate access to medical care and counseling appropriate to the needs of those in custody, recognising any particular needs of persons on the basis of their sexual orientation or gender identity, including with regard to reproductive health, access to HIV/AIDS information and therapy and access to hormonal or other therapy as well as to gender-reassignment treatments where desired;

C. Ensure, to the extent possible, that all prisoners participate in decisions regarding the place of detention appropriate to their sexual orientation and gender identity;

D. Put protective measures in place for all prisoners vulnerable to violence or abuse on the basis of their sexual orientation, gender identity or gender expression and ensure, so far as is reasonably practicable, that such protective measures involve no greater restriction of their rights than is experienced by the general prison population;

E. Ensure that conjugal visits, where permitted, are

granted on an equal basis to all prisoners and detainees, regardless of the gender of their partner;

F. Provide for the independent monitoring of detention facilities by the State as well as by non-governmental organisations including organisations working in the spheres of sexual orientation and gender identity;

G. Undertake programmes of training and awareness raising for prison personnel and all other officials in the public and private sector who are engaged in detention facilities, regarding international human rights standards and principles of equality and nondiscrimination, including in relation to sexual orientation and gender identity.

18. Protection from medical abuses

No person may be forced to undergo any form of medical or psychological treatment, procedure, testing, or be confined to a medical facility, based on sexual orientation or gender identity. Notwithstanding any classifications to the contrary, a person's sexual orientation and gender identity are not, in and of themselves, medical conditions and are not to be treated, cured or suppressed.

States shall:

A. Take all necessary legislative, administrative and other measures to ensure full protection against harmful medical practices based on sexual orientation or gender identity, including on the basis of stereotypes, whether derived from culture or otherwise, regarding conduct, physical appearance or perceived gender norms;

B. Take all necessary legislative, administrative and other measures to ensure that no child's body is irreversibly altered by medical procedures in an attempt to impose a gender identity without the full, free and informed consent of the child in accordance with the age and maturity of the child and guided by the principle that in all actions concerning children, the best interests of the child shall be a primary consideration;

C. Establish child protection mechanisms whereby no child is at risk of, or subjected to, medical abuse;

D. Ensure protection of persons of diverse sexual orientations and gender identities against unethical or involuntary medical procedures or research, including in relation to vaccines, treatments or microbicides for HIV/AIDS or other diseases;

E. Review and amend any health funding provisions or programmes, including those of a development assistance nature, which may promote, facilitate or in any other way render possible such abuses;

F. Ensure that any medical or psychological treatment or counseling does not, explicitly or implicitly, treat sexual orientation and gender identity as medical conditions to be treated, cured or suppressed.

19. The right to freedom of opinion and expression

Everyone has the right to freedom of opinion and expression, regardless of sexual orientation or gender identity. This includes the expression of identity or personhood through speech, deportment, dress, bodily characteristics, choice of name, or any other means, as well as the freedom to seek, receive and impart information and ideas of all kinds, including with regard to human rights, sexual orientation and gender identity, through any medium and regardless of frontiers.

States shall:

A. Take all necessary legislative, administrative and other measures to ensure full enjoyment of freedom of opinion and expression, while respecting the rights and freedoms of others, without discrimination on the basis of sexual orientation or gender identity, including the receipt and imparting of information and ideas concerning sexual orientation and gender identity, as well as related advocacy for legal rights, publication of materials, broadcasting, organisation of or participation in conferences, and dissemination of and access to safer-sex information;

B. Ensure that the outputs and the organisation of media that is State-regulated is pluralistic and nondiscriminatory in respect of issues of sexual orientation and gender identity and that the personnel recruitment and promotion policies of such organisations are non-discriminatory on the basis of sexual orientation or gender identity;

C. Take all necessary legislative, administrative and other measures to ensure the full enjoyment of the right to express identity or personhood, including through speech, deportment, dress, bodily characteristics, choice of name or any other means;

D. Ensure that notions of public order, public morality, public health and public security are not employed to restrict, in a discriminatory manner, any exercise of freedom of opinion and expression that affirms diverse sexual orientations or gender identities;

E. Ensure that the exercise of freedom of opinion and expression does not violate the rights and freedoms of persons of diverse sexual orientations and gender identities;

F. Ensure that all persons, regardless of sexual orientation or gender identity, enjoy equal access to information and ideas, as well as to participation in public debate."

26. The UN bodies, Regional Human Rights Bodies, National Courts, Government Commissions and the Commissions for Human Rights, Council of Europe,

etc. have endorsed the Yogyakarta Principles and have considered them as an important tool for identifying the obligations of States to respect, protect and fulfill the human rights of all persons, regardless of their gender identity. United Nations Committee on Economic, Social and Cultural Rights in its Report of 2009 speaks of gender orientation and gender identity as follows:

"**Sexual orientation and gender identity**–'Other status' as recognized in article 2, paragraph 2, includes sexual orientation. States parties should ensure that a person's sexual orientation is not a barrier to realizing Covenant rights, for example, in accessing survivor's pension rights. In addition, gender identity is recognized as among the prohibited grounds of discrimination, for example, persons who are transgender, transsexual or intersex, often face serious human rights violations, such as harassment in schools or in the workplace."

27. In this respect, reference may also be made to the General Comment No.2 of the Committee on Torture and Article 2 of the Convention against Torture and Other Cruel, Inhuman or Degrading Treatment or Punishment in 2008 and also the General Comment No.20 of the Committee on Elimination of Discrimination against Woman, responsible for the implementation of the Convention on the Elimination of All Forms of Discrimination against Woman, 1979 and 2010 report.

SRS and Foreign Judgments

28. Various countries have given recognition to the gender identity of such persons, mostly, in cases where transsexual persons started asserting their rights after undergoing SRS of their re-assigned sex. In Corbett v. Corbett (1970) 2 All ER 33, the Court in England was concerned with the gender of a male to female transsexual in the context of the validity of a marriage. Ormrod, J. in that case took the view that the law should adopt the chromosomal, gonadal and genital tests and if all three are congruent, that should determine a person's sex for the purpose of marriage. Learned Judge expressed the view that any operative intervention should be ignored and the biological sexual constitution of an individual is fixed at birth, at the latest, and cannot be changed either by the natural development of organs of the opposite sex or by medical or surgical means. Later, in R v. Tan (1983) QB 1053, 1063-1064, the Court of Appeal applied Corbett approach in the context of criminal law. The Court upheld convictions which were imposed on Gloria Greaves, a postoperative male to female transsexual, still being in law, a man.

29. Corbett principle was not found favour by various other countries, like New Zealand, Australia etc. and also attracted much criticism, from the medical profession. It was felt that the application of the Corbett approach would lead to a substantial different outcome in cases

of a post operative inter-sexual person and a post operative transsexual person. In New Zealand in *Attorney-General v. Otahuhu Family Court* (1995) 1 NZLR 603, Justice Ellis noted that once a transsexual person has undergone surgery, he or she is no longer able to operate in his or her original sex. It was held that there is no social advantage in the law for not recognizing the validity of the marriage of a transsexual in the sex of reassignment. The Court held that an adequate test is whether the person in question has undergone surgical and medical procedures that have effectively given the person the physical conformation of a person of a specified sex. In *Re Kevin (Validity of Marriage of Transsexual)* (2001) Fam CA 1074, in an Australian case, Chisholm J., held that there is no 'formulaic solution' to determine the sex of an individual for the purpose of the law of marriage. It was held that all relevant matters need to be considered, including the person's life experiences and self perception. Full Court of the Federal Family Court in the year 2003 approved the above-mentioned judgment holding that in the relevant Commonwealth marriage statute the words 'man' and 'woman' should be given their ordinary, everyday contemporary meaning and that the word 'man' includes a post operative female to male transsexual person. The Full Court also held that there was a biological basis for trans sexualism and that there was no reason to exclude the psyche as one of the relevant factors in determining sex and gender. The judgment Attorney-General for the Commonwealth & "Kevin and Jennifer" & Human Rights and Equal Opportunity Commission is reported in (2003) Fam CA 94.

30. Lockhart, J. in Secretary, Department of Social Security v. "SRA", (1993) 43 FCR 299 and Mathews, J. in *R v. Harris & McGuiness* (1988) 17 NSWLR 158, made an exhaustive review of the various decisions with regard to the question of recognition to be accorded by Courts to the gender of a transsexual person who had undertaken a surgical procedure. The Courts generally in New Zealand held that the decision in Corbett v. Corbett (supra) and R v. Tan (supra) which applied a purely biological test, should 32 not be followed. In fact, Lockhart J. in SRA observed that the development in surgical and medical techniques in the field of sexual reassignment, together with indications of changing social attitudes towards transsexuals, would indicate that generally they should not be regarded merely as a matter of chromosomes, which is purely a psychological question, one of self-perception, and partly a social question, how society perceives the individual.

31. *A.B. v. Western Australia* (2011) HCA 42 was a case concerned with the Gender Reassignment Act, 2000. In that Act, a person who had undergone a reassignment procedure could apply to Gender Reassignment Board

for the issue of a recognition certificate. Under Section 15 of that Act, before issuing the certificate, the Board had to be satisfied, inter alia, that the applicant believed his or her true gender was the person's reassigned gender and had adopted the lifestyle and gender characteristics of that gender. Majority of Judges agreed with Lockhart, J. in SRA that gender should not be regarded merely as a matter of chromosomes, but partly a psychological question, one of self-perception, and partly a social question, how society perceives the individual.

32. The House of Lords in *Bellinger v. Bellinger* (2003) 2 All ER 593 was dealing with the question of a transsexual. In that case, Mrs. Bellinger was born on 7th September, 1946. At birth, she was correctly classified and registered as male. However, she felt more inclined to be a female. Despite her inclinations, and under some pressure, in 1967 she married a woman and at that time she was 21 years old. Marriage broke down and parties separated in 1971 and got divorce in the year 1975. Mrs. Bellinger dressed and lived like a woman and when she married Mr. Bellinger, he was fully aware of her background and throughout had been supportive to her. Mr. and Mrs. Bellinger since marriage lived happily as husband and wife and presented themselves in that fashion to the outside world. Mrs. Bellinger's primary claim was for a declaration under Section 55 of the Family Law Act, 1986 that her marriage to Mr. Bellinger

in 1981 was "at its inception valid marriage". The House of Lords rejected the claim and dismissed the appeal. Certainly, the "psychological factor" has not been given much prominence in determination of the claim of Mrs. Bellinger.

33. The High Court of Kuala Lumpur in *Re JG, JG v. Pengarah Jabatan Pendaftaran Negara* (2006) 1 MLJ 90, was considering the question as to whether an application to amend or correct gender status stated in National Registration Identity Card could be allowed after a person has undergone SRS. It was a case where the plaintiff was born as a male, but felt more inclined to be a woman. In 1996 at Hospital Siroros she underwent a gender reassignment and got the surgery done for changing the sex from male to female and then she lived like a woman. She applied to authorities to change her name and also for a declaration of her gender as female, but her request was not favourably considered, but still treated as a male. She sought a declaration from the Court that she be declared as a female and that the Registration Department be directed to change the last digit of her identity card to a digit that reflects a female gender. The Malaysian Court basically applied the principle laid down in Corbett (supra), however, both the prayers sought for were granted, after noticing that the medical men have spoken that the plaintiff is a female and they have considered the sex change of the

plaintiff as well as her "psychological aspect". The Court noticed that she feels like a woman, lives like one, behaves as one, has her physical body attuned to one, and most important of all, her "psychological thinking" is that of a woman.

34. The Court of Appeal, New South Wales was called upon to decide the question whether the Registrar of Births, Deaths and Marriages has the power under the Births, Deaths and Marriages Act, 1995 to register a change of sex of a person and the sex recorded on the register to "non-specific" or "non-specified". The appeal was allowed and the matter was remitted back to the Tribunal for a fresh consideration in accordance with law, after laying down the law on the subject. The judgment is reported as *Norrie v. NSW Registrar of Births, Deaths and Marriages* (2013) NSWCA 145. While disposing of the appeal, the Court held as follows:

"The consequence is that the Appeal Panel (and the Tribunal and the Registrar) were in error in construing the power in S.32DC(1) as limiting the Registrar to registering a person's change of sex as only male or female. An error in the construction of the statutory provision granting the power to register a person's change of sex is an error on a question of law. Collector of Customs v. Pozzolanic Enterprises Pty. Ltd. [1993] FCA 322; (1993) 43 FCR 280 at 287. This is so notwithstanding that the determination of the common understanding of a general word used in the statutory provision is a question of fact. The Appeal Panel (and the Tribunal and the Registrar) erred in determining that the current ordinary meaning of the word "sex" is limited to the character of being either male or female. That involved an error on a question of fact. But the Appeal Panel's error in arriving at the common understanding of the word "sex" was associated with its error in construction of the effect of the statutory provision of S.32DC (and also of S.32DA), and accordingly is of law: Hope v. Bathurst City Council [1980] HCA 16, (1980) 144 CLR 1 at 10."

35. In *Christine Goodwin v. United Kingdom* (Application No.28957/95 - Judgment dated 11th July, 2002), the European Court of Human Rights examined an application alleging violation of Articles 8, 12, 13 and 14 of the Convention for Protection of Human Rights and Fundamental Freedoms, 1997 in respect of the legal status of transsexuals in UK and particularly their treatment in the sphere of employment, social security, pensions and marriage. Applicant in that case had a tendency to dress as a woman from early childhood and underwent aversion therapy in 1963-64. In the mid-1960s she was diagnosed as a transsexual. Though she married a woman and they had four children, her

inclination was that her "brain sex" did not fit her body. From that time until 1984 she dressed as a man for work but as a woman in her free time. In January, 1985, the applicant began treatment at the Gender Identity Clinic. In October, 1986, she underwent surgery to shorten her vocal chords. In August, 1987, she was accepted on the waiting list for gender re-assignment surgery and later underwent that surgery at a National Health Service hospital. The applicant later divorced her former wife. She claimed between 1990 and 1992 she was sexually harassed by colleagues at work, followed by other human rights violations. The Court after referring to various provisions and Conventions held as follows:

"Nonetheless, the very essence of the Convention is respect for human dignity and human freedom. Under Article 8 of the Convention in particular, where the notion of personal autonomy is an important principle underlying the interpretation of its guarantees, protection is given to the personal sphere of each individuals, including the right to establish details of their identity as individual human beings (see, inter alia, Pretty v. the United Kingdom no.2346/02, judgment of 29 April 2002, 62, and Mikulic v. Croatia, no.53176/99, judgment of 7 February 2002, 53, both to be published in ECHR 2002...). In the twenty first century the right of transsexuals to personal development and to physical and moral security in the full sense enjoyed by others in society cannot be regarded as a matter of controversy requiring the lapse of time to cast clearer light on the issues involved. In short, the unsatisfactory situation in which postoperative transsexuals live in an intermediate zone as not quite one gender or the other is no longer sustainable."

36. The European Court of Human Rights in the case of *Van Kuck v. Germany (Application No.35968/97 – Judgment dated 12.9.2003)* dealt with the application alleging that German Court's decisions refusing the applicant's claim for reimbursement of gender reassignment measures and the related proceedings were in breach of her rights to a fair trial and of her right to respect for her private life and that they amounted to discrimination on the ground of her particular "psychological situation". Reliance was placed on Articles 6, 8, 13 and 14 of the Convention for Protection of Human Rights and Fundamental Freedoms, 1997. The Court held that the concept of "private life" covers the physical and psychological integrity of a person, which can sometimes embrace aspects of an individual's physical and social identity. For example, gender identifications, name and sexual orientation and sexual life fall within the personal sphere protected by Article 8. The Court also held that the notion of personal identity is an

important principle underlying the interpretation of various guaranteed rights and the very essence of the Convention being respect for human dignity and human freedom, protection is given to the right of transsexuals to personal development and to physical and moral security.

37. Judgments referred to above are mainly related to transsexuals, who, whilst belonging physically to one sex, feel convinced that they belong to the other, seek to achieve a more integrated unambiguous identity by undergoing medical and surgical operations to adapt their physical characteristic to their psychological nature. When we examine the rights of transsexual persons, who have undergone SRS, the test to be applied is not the "Biological test", but the "Psychological test", because psychological factor and thinking of transsexual has to be given primacy than binary notion of gender of that person. Seldom people realize the discomfort, distress and psychological trauma, they undergo and many of them undergo "Gender Dysphoria' which may lead to mental disorder. Discrimination faced by this group in our society, is rather unimaginable and their rights have to be protected, irrespective of chromosomal sex, genitals, assigned birth sex, or implied gender role. Rights of transgenders, pure and simple, like Hijras, eunuchs, etc. have also to be examined, so also their right to remain as a third gender as well as their physical and

psychological integrity. Before addressing those aspects further, we may also refer to few legislations enacted in other countries recognizing their rights.

Legislations in Other Countries on TGs

38. We notice, following the trend, in the international human rights law, many countries have enacted laws for recognizing rights of transsexual persons, who have undergone either partial/complete SRS, including United Kingdom, Netherlands, Germany, Australia, Canada, Argentina, etc. United Kingdom has passed the General Recommendation Act, 2004, following the judgment in Christine Goodwin (supra) passed by the European Courts of Human Rights. The Act is all encompassing as not only does it provide legal recognition to the acquired gender of a person, but it also lays down provisions highlighting the consequences of the newly acquired gender status on their legal rights and entitlements in various aspects such as marriage, parentage, succession, social security and pensions etc. One of the notable features of the Act is that it is not necessary that a person needs to have undergone or in the process of undergoing a SRS to apply under the Act. Reference in this connection may be made to the Equality Act, 2010 (UK) which has consolidated, repealed and replaced around nine different anti-discrimination legislations including the Sex

Discrimination Act, 1986. The Act defines certain characteristics to be "protected characteristics" and no one shall be discriminated or treated less favourably on grounds that the person possesses one or more of the "protected characteristics". The Act also imposes duties on Public Bodies to eliminate all kinds of discrimination, harassment and victimization. Gender reassignment has been declared as one of the protected characteristics under the Act, of course, only the transsexuals i.e. those who are proposing to undergo, is undergoing or has undergone the process of the gender reassignment are protected under the Act.

39. In Australia, there are two Acts dealing with the gender identity, (1) Sex Discrimination Act, 1984; and (ii) Sex Discrimination Amendment (Sexual Orientation, Gender Identity and Intersex Status) Act, 2013 (Act 2013). Act 2013 amends the Sex Discrimination Act, 1984. Act 2013 defines gender identity as the appearance or mannerisms or other gender-related characteristics of a person (whether by way of medical intervention or not) with or without regard to the person's designated sex at birth.

40. Sections 5(A), (B) and (C) of the 2013 Act have some relevance and the same are extracted herein below:

"**5A Discrimination on the ground of sexual orientation**- (1) For the purposes of this Act, a person (the discriminator) discriminates against another person (the aggrieved person) on the ground of the aggrieved person's sexual orientation if, by reason of:

(a) the aggrieved person's sexual orientation; or (b) a characteristic that appertains generally to persons who have the same sexual orientation as the aggrieved person; or (c) a characteristic that is generally imputed to persons who have the same sexual orientation as the aggrieved person; the discriminator treats the aggrieved person less favourably than, in circumstances that are the same or are not materially different, the discriminator treats or would treat a person who has a different sexual orientation.

(2) For the purposes of this Act, a person (the discriminator) discriminates against another person (the aggrieved person) on the ground of the aggrieved person's sexual orientation if the discriminator imposes, or proposes to impose, a condition, requirement or practice that has, or is likely to have, the effect of disadvantaging persons who have the same sexual orientation as the aggrieved person.

(3) This section has effect subject to sections 7B and 7D. 5B Discrimination on the ground of gender identity (1) For the purposes of this Act, a person (the discriminator) discriminates against another

person (the aggrieved person) on the ground of the aggrieved person's gender identity if, by reason of: (a) the aggrieved person's gender identity; or (b) a characteristic that appertains generally to persons who have the same gender identity as the aggrieved person; or (c) a characteristic that is generally imputed to persons who have the same gender identity as the aggrieved person; the discriminator treats the aggrieved person less favourably than, in circumstances that are the same or are not materially different, the discriminator treats or would treat a person who has a different gender identity. (2) For the purposes of this Act, a person (the discriminator) discriminates against another person (the aggrieved person) on the ground of the aggrieved person's gender identity if the discriminator imposes, or proposes to impose, a condition, requirement or practice that has, or is likely to have, the effect of disadvantaging persons who have the same gender identity as the aggrieved person. (3) This section has effect subject to sections 7B and 7D.

"5C Discrimination on the ground of intersex status- (1) For the purposes of this Act, a person (the discriminator) discriminates against another person (the aggrieved person) on the ground of the aggrieved person's intersex status if, by reason of: (a) the aggrieved person's intersex status; or (b) a characteristic that appertains generally to persons of intersex status; or (c) a characteristic that is generally imputed to persons of intersex status; the discriminator treats the aggrieved person less favourably than, in circumstances that are the same or are not materially different, the discriminator treats or would treat a person who is not of intersex status. (2) For the purposes of this Act, a person (the discriminator) discriminates against another person (the aggrieved person) on the ground of the aggrieved person's intersex status if the discriminator imposes, or proposes to impose, a condition, requirement or practice that has, or is likely to have, the effect of disadvantaging persons of intersex status. (3) This section has effect subject to sections 7B and 7D." Various other precautions have also been provided under the Act.

41. We may in this respect also refer to the European Union Legislations on transsexuals. Recital 3 of the Preamble to the Directive 2006/54/EC of European Parliament and the Council of 5 July 2006 makes an explicit reference to discrimination based on gender reassignment for the first time in European Union Law. Recital 3 reads as under:

   "The Court of Justice has held that the scope of the principle of equal treatment for men and women cannot be confined to the prohibition of discrimination based on the fact that a person is of one or other sex. In view of this purpose and the nature of the rights which it seeks to safeguard, it also applies to discrimination arising from the gender reassignment of a person."

42. European Parliament also adopted a resolution on discrimination against transsexuals on 12th September, 1989 and called upon the Member States to take steps for the protection of transsexual persons and to pass legislation to further that end. Following that Hungary has enacted Equal Treatment and the Promotion of Equal Opportunities Act, 2003, which includes sexual identity as one of the grounds of discrimination. 2010 paper on 'Transgender Persons' Rights in the EU Member States prepared by the Policy Department of the European Parliament presents the specific situation of transgender people in 27 Member States of the European Union. In the United States of America some of the laws enacted by the States are inconsistent with each other. The Federal Law which provides protection to transgenders is The Matthew Shepard and James Byrd. Jr. Hate Crimes Prevention Act, 2009, which expands the scope of the 1969 United States Federal Hate-crime Law by including offences motivated by actual or perceived gender identity. Around 15 States and District of Colombia in the United States have legislations which prohibit discrimination on grounds

of gender identity and expression. Few States have issued executive orders prohibiting discrimination.

43. The Parliament of South Africa in the year 2003, enacted Alteration of Sex Description and Sex Status Act, 2003, which permits transgender persons who have undergone gender reassignment or people whose sexual characteristics have evolved naturally or an inter sexed person to apply to the Director General of the National Department of Home Affairs for alteration of his/her sex description in the birth register, though the legislation does not contemplate a more inclusive definition of transgenders.

44. The Senate of Argentina in the year 2012 passed a law on Gender Identity that recognizes right by all persons to the recognition of their gender identity as well as free development of their person according to their gender identity and can also request that their recorded sex be amended along with the changes in first name and image, whenever they do not agree with the self-perceived gender identity. Not necessary that they seemed to prove that a surgical procedure for total or partial genital reassignment, hormonal therapies or any other psychological or medical treatment had taken place. Article 12 deals with dignified treatment, respecting the gender identity adopted by the individual, even though the first name is different from the one recorded in their national identity documents. Further laws also provide

that whenever requested by the individual, the adopted first name must be used for summoning, recording, filing, calling and any other procedure or service in public and private spaces.

45. In Germany, a new law has come into force on 5th November, 2013, which allows the parents to register the sex of the children as 'not specified' in the case of children with intersex variation. According to Article 22, Section 3 of the German Civil Statutes Act reads as follows:

"If a child can be assigned to neither the female nor the male sex then the child has to be named without a specification."

The law has also added a category of X, apart from "M" and "F" under the classification of gender in the passports.

The Indian Scenario

46. We have referred exhaustively to the various judicial pronouncements and legislations on the international arena to highlight the fact that the recognition of "sex identity gender" of persons, and "guarantee to equality and non-discrimination" on the ground of gender identity or expression is increasing and gaining acceptance in international law and, therefore, be applied in India as well.

47. The historical background of Transgenders in India has already been dealth in the earlier part of this Judgment indicating that they were once treated with great respect, at least in the past, though not in the present. We can perceive a wide range of transgender related identities, cultures or experiences which are generally as follows:

"Hijras:

Hijras are biological males who reject their 'masculine' identity in due course of time to identify either 48 as women, or "not-men", or "in-between man and woman", or "neither man nor woman". Hijras can be considered as the western equivalent of transgender/transsexual (male-to-female) persons but Hijras have a long tradition/culture and have strong social ties formalized through a ritual called "reet" (becoming a member of Hijra community). There are regional variations in the use of terms referred to Hijras. For example, Kinnars (Delhi) and Aravanis (Tamil Nadu). Hijras may earn through their traditional work: 'Badhai' (clapping their hands and asking for alms), blessing newborn babies, or dancing in ceremonies. Some proportion of Hijras engage in sex work for lack of other job opportunities, while some may be self-employed or work for non-governmental organisations." (See UNDP India Report (December, 2010).

Eunuch:

Eunuch refers to an emasculated male and intersexed to a person whose genitals are ambiguously male-like at birth, but this is discovered the child previously assigned to the male sex, would be recategorized as intesexexd – as a Hijra.

"Aravanis and 'Thirunangi':

Hijras in Tamil Nadu identify as "Aravani". Tamil Nadu Aravanigal Welfare Board, a state government's initiative under the Department of Social Welfare defines Aravanis as biological males who self-identify themselves as a woman trapped in a male's body. Some Aravani activists want the public and media to use the term 'Thirunangi' to refer to Aravanis.

Kothi:

Kothis are a heterogeneous group. 'Kothis' can be described as biological males who show varying degrees of 'femininity' – which may be situational. Some proportion of Kothis have bisexual behavior and get married to a woman. Kothis are generally of lower socioeconomic status and some engage in sex work for survival. Some proportion of Hijra-identified people may also identify themselves as 'Kothis'. But not all Kothi identified people identify themselves as transgender or Hijras.

Jogtas/Jogappas:

Jogtas or Jogappas are those persons who are dedicated to and serve as a servant of goddess Renukha Devi (Yellamma) whose temples are present in Maharashtra and Karnataka. 'Jogta' refers to male servant of that Goddess and 'Jogti' refers to female servant (who is also sometimes referred to as 'Devadasi'). One can become a 'Jogta' (or Jogti) if it is part of their family tradition or if one finds a 'Guru' (or 'Pujari') who accepts him/her as a 'Chela' or 'Shishya' (disciple). Sometimes, the term 'Jogti Hijras' is used to denote those male-to-female transgender persons who are devotees/servants of Goddess Renukha Devi and who are also in the Hijra communities. This term is used to differentiate them from 'Jogtas' who are heterosexuals and who may or may not dress in woman's attire when they worship the Goddess. Also, that term differentiates them from 'Jogtis' who are biological females dedicated to the Goddess. However, 'Jogti Hijras' may refer to themselves as 'Jogti' (female pronoun) or Hijras, and even sometimes as 'Jogtas'.

Shiv-Shakthis:

Shiv-Shakthis are considered as males who are possessed by or particularly close to a goddess and who have feminine gender expression. Usually, ShivShakthis are inducted into the Shiv-Shakti community by senior gurus, who teach them the norms, customs, and rituals to be observed by them. In a ceremony, ShivShakthis are married to a sword that represents male power or Shiva (deity). Shiv-Shakthis thus become the bride of the sword. Occasionally, Shiv-Shakthis crossdress and use accessories and ornaments that are generally/socially meant for women. Most people in this community belong to lower socio-economic status and earn for their living as astrologers, soothsayers, and spiritual healers; some also seek alms." (See Serena Nanda, Wadsworth Publishing Company, Second Edition (1999)

48. Transgender people, as a whole, face multiple forms of oppression in this country. Discrimination is so large and pronounced, especially in the field of health care, employment, education, leave aside social exclusion. A detailed study was conducted by the United Nations Development Programme (UNDP – India) and submitted a report in December, 2010 on Hijras/ transgenders in India: "HIV Human Rights and Social Exclusion". The Report states that the HIV Human Immunodeficiency Virus and Sexually Transmitted Infections (STI) is now increasingly seen in Hijras/ transgenders population. The estimated size of men who have sex with men (MSM) and male sex workers population in India (latter presumably includes Hijras/ TG communities) is 2,352,133 and 235,213 respectively. It was stated that no reliable estimates are

available for Hijras/TG women. HIV prevalence among MSM population was 7.4% against the overall adult HIV prevalence of 0.36%. It was stated recently Hijras/ TG people were included under the category of MSM in HIV sentinel sero surveillance. It is also reported in recent studies that Hijras/TG women have indicated a very high HIV prevalence (17.5% to 41%) among them. Study conducted by NACO also highlights a pathetic situation. Report submitted by NACI, NACP IV Working Group Hijras TG dated 5.5.2011 would indicate that transgenders are extremely vulnerable to HIV. Both the reports highlight the extreme necessity of taking emergent steps to improve their sexual health, mental health and also address the issue of social exclusion.

49. The UNDP in its report has made the following recommendations, which are as under:

"Multiple problems are faced by Hijras/TG, which necessitate a variety of solutions and actions. While some actions require immediate implementation such as introducing Hijra/TG-specific social welfare schemes, some actions need to be taken on a long-term basis changing the negative attitude of the general public and increasing accurate knowledge about Hijra/TG communities. The required changes need to be reflected in policies and laws; attitude of the government, general public and health care providers; and health care systems and practice. Key recommendations include the following:

1. Address the gape in NACP-III: establish HIV sentinel serosurveillance sites for Hijras/TG at strategic locations; conduct operations research to design and fine-tune culturally-relevant package of HIV prevention and care interventions for Hijras/TG; provide financial support for the formation of CBOs run by Hijras/TG; and build the capacity of CBOs to implement effective rogrammes.

2. Move beyond focusing on individual-level HIV prevention activities to address the structural determinants of risks and mitigate the impact of risks. For example, mental health counseling, crisis intervention (crisis in relation to suicidal tendencies, police harassment and arrests, support following sexual and physical violence), addressing alcohol and drug abuse, and connecting to livelihood programs all need to be part of the HIV interventions.

3. Train health care providers to be competent and sensitive in providing health care services (including 52 STI and HIV-related services) to Hijras/TG as well as develop and monitor implementation of guidelines related to gender transition and sex reassignment surgery (SRS).

4. Clarify the ambiguous legal status of sex reassignment surgery and provide gender transition

and SRS services (with proper pre-and post-operation/transition counseling) for free in public hospitals in various parts in India.

5. Implement stigma and discrimination reduction measures at various settings through a variety of ways: mass media awareness for the general public to focused training and sensitization for police and health care providers.

6. Develop action steps toward taking a position on legal recognition of gender identity of Hijras/TG need to be taken in consultation with Hijras/TG and other key stakeholders. Getting legal recognition and avoiding ambiguities in the current procedures that issue identity documents to Hijras/TGs are required as they are connected to basic civil rights such as access to health and public services, right to vote, right to contest elections, right to education, inheritance rights, and marriage and child adoption.

7. Open up the existing Social Welfare Schemes for needy Hijras/TG and create specific welfare schemes to address the basic needs of Hijras/TG including housing and employment needs.

8. Ensure greater involvement of vulnerable communities including Hijras/TG women in policy formulation and program development."

50. Social exclusion and discrimination on the ground of gender stating that one does not conform to the binary gender (male/female) does prevail in India. Discussion on gender identity including self-identification of gender of male/female or as transgender mostly focuses on those persons who are assigned male sex at birth, whether one talks of Hijra transgender, woman or male or male to female transgender persons, while concern voiced by those who are identified as female to male trans-sexual persons often not properly addressed. Female to male unlike Hijra/ transgender persons are not quite visible in public unlike Hijra/transgender persons. Many of them, however, do experience violence and discrimination because of their sexual orientation or gender identity.

India to follow International Conventions

51. International Conventions and norms are significant for the purpose of interpretation of gender equality. Article 1 of the Universal declaration on Human Rights, 1948, states that all human-beings are born free and equal in dignity and rights. Article 3 of the Universal Declaration of Human Rights states that everyone has a right to life, liberty and security of person. Article 6 of the International Covenant on Civil and Political Rights, 1966 affirms that every human-being has the inherent right to life, which right shall be protected by law and

no one shall be arbitrarily deprived of his life. Article 5 of the Universal Declaration of Human Rights and Article 7 of the International Covenant on Civil and Political Rights provide that no one shall be subjected to torture or to cruel inhuman or degrading treatment or punishment. United Nations Convention against Torture and Other Cruel Inhuman and Degrading Treatment or Punishment (dated 24th January, 2008) specifically deals with protection of individuals and groups made vulnerable by discrimination or marginalization. Para 21 of the Convention states that States are obliged to protect from torture or ill-treatment all persons regardless of sexual orientation or transgender identity and to prohibit, prevent and provide redress for torture and ill-treatment in all contests of State custody or control. Article 12 of the Universal Declaration of Human Rights and Article 17 of the International Covenant on Civil and Political Rights state that no one shall be subjected to "arbitrary or unlawful interference with his privacy, family, home or correspondence".

52. The above-mentioned International Human Rights instruments which are being followed by various countries in the world are aimed to protect the human rights of transgender people since it 55 has been noticed that transgenders/transsexuals often face serious human rights violations, such as harassment in work place, hospitals, places of public conveniences, market places,

theaters, railway stations, bus stands, and so on.

53. Indian Law, on the whole, only recognizes the paradigm of binary genders of male and female, based on a person's sex assigned by birth, which permits gender system, including the law relating to marriage, adoption, inheritance, succession and taxation and welfare legislations. We have exhaustively referred to various articles contained in the Universal Declaration of Human Rights, 1948, the International Covenant on Economic, Social and Cultural Rights, 1966, the International Covenant on Civil and Political Rights, 1966 as well as the Yogyakarta principles. Reference was also made to legislations enacted in other countries dealing with rights of persons of transgender community. Unfortunately we have no legislation in this country dealing with the rights of transgender community. Due to the absence of suitable legislation protecting the rights of the members of the transgender community, they are facing discrimination in various areas and hence the necessity to follow the International Conventions to which India is a party and to give due respect to other non-binding International Conventions and principles. Constitution makers could not have envisaged that each and every human activity be guided, controlled, recognized or safeguarded by laws made by the legislature. Article 21 has been incorporated to safeguard those rights and a constitutional Court cannot be a mute spectator when

those rights are violated, but is expected to safeguard those rights knowing the pulse and feeling of that community, though a minority, especially when their rights have gained universal recognition and acceptance.

54. Article 253 of the Constitution of India states that the Parliament has the power to make any law for the whole or any part of the territory of India for implementing any treaty, agreement or convention. Generally, therefore, a legislation is required for implementing the international conventions, unlike the position in the United States of America where the rules of international law are applied by the municipal courts on the theory of their implied adoption by the State, as a part of its own municipal law. Article VI, Cl. (2) of the U.S. Constitution reads as follows:

   "........all treaties made, or which shall be made, under the authority of the united States, shall be the supreme law of the land, and the judges in every State shall be bound thereby, anything in the Constitution or laws of any State to the contrary not-withstanding."

55. In the United States, however, it is open to the courts to supersede or modify international law in its application or it may be controlled by the treaties entered into by the United States. But, till an Act of Congress is passed, the Court is bound by the law of nations,

which is part of the law of the land. Such a 'supremacy clause' is absent in our Constitution. Courts in India would apply the rules of International law according to the principles of comity of Nations, unless they are overridden by clear rules of domestic law. See: Gramophone Company of India Ltd. v. Birendra Bahadur Pandey (1984) 2 SCC 534 and Tractor Export v. Tarapore & Co. (1969) 3 SCC 562, Mirza Ali Akbar Kashani v. United Arab Republic (1966) 1 SCR 391.

56. In the case of *Jolly George Varghese v. Bank of Cochin* (1980) 2 SCC 360, the Court applied the above principle in respect of the International Covenant on Civil and Political Rights, 1966 as well as in connection with the Universal Declaration of Human Rights. India has ratified the above mentioned covenants; hence, those covenants can be used by the municipal courts as an aid to the Interpretation of Statutes by applying the Doctrine of Harmonization. But, certainly, if the Indian law is not in conflict with the International covenants, particularly pertaining to human rights, to which India is a party, the domestic court can apply those principles in the Indian conditions. The Interpretation of International Conventions is governed by Articles 31 and 32 of the Vienna Convention on the Law of Treaties of 1969.

57. Article 51 of the Directive Principles of State Policy,

which falls under Part IV of the Indian Constitution, reads as under:

"Art. 51. The State shall endeavour to – (a)promote international peace and security; (b) maintain just and honourable relations between nations; (c)Foster respect for international law and treaty obligation in the dealings of organised peoples with one another; and (d)Encourage settlement of international disputes by arbitration."

58. Article 51, as already indicated, has to be read along with Article 253 of the Constitution. If the parliament has made any legislation which is in conflict with the international law, then Indian Courts are bound to give effect to the Indian Law, rather than the international law. However, in the absence of a contrary legislation, municipal courts in India would respect the rules of international law. In *His Holiness Kesavananda Bharati Sripadavalvaru v. State of Kerala* (1973) 4 SCC 225, it was stated that in view of Article 51 of the Constitution, the Court must interpret language of the Constitution, if not intractable, in the light of United Nations Charter and the solemn declaration subscribed to it by India. In *Apparel Export Promotion Council v. A. K. Chopra* (1999) 1 SCC 759, it was pointed out that domestic courts are under an obligation to give due regard to the international conventions and norms for construing the domestic laws, more so, when there is no inconsistency

between them and there is a void in domestic law. Reference may also be made to the Judgments of this Court in *Githa Hariharan (Ms) and another v. Reserve Bank of India* and another (1999) 2 SCC 228, *R.D. Upadhyay v. State of Andhra Pradesh and others* (2007) 15 SCC 337 and *People's Union for Civil Liberties v. Union of India and another* (2005) 2 SCC 436.

59. In *Vishaka and others v. State of Rajasthan and Others* (1997) 6 SCC 241, this Court under Article 141 laid down various guidelines to prevent sexual harassment of women in working places, and to enable gender equality relying on Articles 11, 24 and general recommendations 22, 23 and 24 of the Convention on the Elimination of All Forms of Discrimination against Women. Any international convention not inconsistent with the fundamental rights and in harmony with its spirit must be read into those provisions, e.g., Articles 14, 15, 19 and 21 of the Constitution to enlarge the meaning and content thereof and to promote the object of constitutional guarantee.

60. The principles discussed hereinbefore on TGs and the International Conventions, including Yogyakarta principles, which we have found not inconsistent with the various fundamental rights guaranteed under the Indian Constitution, must be recognized and followed, which has sufficient legal and historical justification in our country.

Article 14 and Transgenders

61. Article 14 of the Constitution of India states that the State shall not deny to "any person" equality before the law or the equal protection of the laws within the territory of India. Equality includes the full and equal enjoyment of all rights and freedom. Right to equality has been declared as the basic feature of the Constitution and treatment of equals as unequals or unequals as equals will be violative of the basic structure of the Constitution. Article 14 of the Constitution also ensures equal protection and hence a positive obligation on the State to ensure equal protection of laws by bringing in necessary social and economic changes, so that everyone including TGs may enjoy equal protection of laws and 61 nobody is denied such protection. Article 14 does not restrict the word 'person' and its application only to male or female. Hijras/transgender persons who are neither male/female fall within the expression 'person' and, hence, entitled to legal protection of laws in all spheres of State activity, including employment, healthcare, education as well as equal civil and citizenship rights, as enjoyed by any other citizen of this country.

62. The petitioners have asserted as well as demonstrated on facts and figures supported by relevant materials that despite constitutional guarantee of equality, Hijras/ transgender persons have been facing extreme

discrimination in all spheres of the society. Non-recognition of the identity of Hijras/transgender persons denies them equal protection of law, thereby leaving them extremely vulnerable to harassment, violence and sexual assault in public spaces, at home and in jail, also by the police. Sexual assault, including molestation, rape, forced anal and oral sex, gang rape and stripping is being committed with impunity and there are reliable statistics and materials to support such activities. Further, non-recognition of identity of Hijras /transgender persons results in them facing extreme discrimination in all spheres of society, especially in the field of employment, education, healthcare etc. Hijras/transgender persons face huge discrimination in access to public spaces like restaurants, cinemas, shops, malls etc. Further, access to public toilets is also a serious problem they face quite often. Since, there are no separate toilet facilities for Hijras/transgender persons, they have to use male toilets where they are prone to sexual assault and harassment. Discrimination on the ground of sexual orientation or gender identity, therefore, impairs equality before law and equal protection of law and violates Article 14 of the Constitution of India.

Articles 15 and 16 and Transgenders

63. Articles 15 and 16 prohibit discrimination against any citizen on certain enumerated grounds, including the ground of 'sex'. In fact, both the Articles prohibit all

forms of gender bias and gender based discrimination.

64. Article 15 states that the State shall not discriminate against any citizen, inter alia, on the ground of sex, with regard to (a) access to shops, public restaurants, hotels and places of public entertainment; or (b) use of wells, tanks, bathing ghats, roads and places of public resort maintained wholly or partly out of State funds or dedicated to the use of the general public. The requirement of taking affirmative action for the advancement of any socially and educationally backward classes of citizens is also provided in this Article.

65. Article 16 states that there shall be equality of opportunities for all the citizens in matters relating to employment or appointment to any office under the State. Article 16 (2) of the Constitution of India reads as follows:

"16(2). No citizen shall, on grounds only of religion, race, caste, sex, descent, place of birth, residence or any of them, be ineligible for, or discriminated against in respect or, any employment or office under the State."

Article 16 not only prohibits discrimination on the ground of sex in public employment, but also imposes a duty on the State to ensure that all citizens are treated equally in matters relating to employment and appointment by the State.

66. Articles 15 and 16 sought to prohibit discrimination on the basis of sex, recognizing that sex discrimination is a historical fact and needs to be addressed. Constitution makers, it can be gathered, gave emphasis to the fundamental right against sex discrimination so as to prevent the direct or indirect attitude to treat people differently, for the reason of not being in conformity with stereotypical generalizations of binary genders. Both gender and biological attributes constitute distinct components of sex. Biological characteristics, of course, include genitals, chromosomes and secondary sexual features, but gender attributes include one's self image, the deep psychological or emotional sense of sexual identity and character. The discrimination on the ground of 'sex' under Articles 15 and 16, therefore, includes discrimination on the ground of gender identity. The expression 'sex' used in Articles 15 and 16 is not just limited to biological sex of male or female, but intended to include people who consider themselves to be neither male or female.

67. TGs have been systematically denied the rights under Article 15(2) that is not to be subjected to any disability, liability, restriction or condition in regard to access to public places. TGs have also not been afforded special provisions envisaged under Article 15(4) for the advancement of the socially and educationally backward classes (SEBC) of citizens, which they are, and hence

legally entitled and eligible to get the benefits of SEBC. State is bound to take some affirmative action for their advancement so that the injustice done to them for centuries could be remedied. TGs are also entitled to enjoy economic, social, cultural and political rights without discrimination, because forms of discrimination on the ground of gender are violative of fundamental freedoms and human rights. TGs have also been denied rights under Article 16(2) and discriminated against in respect of employment or office under the State on the ground of sex. TGs are also entitled to reservation in the matter of appointment, as envisaged under Article 16(4) of the Constitution. State is bound to take affirmative action to give them due representation in public services.

68. Articles 15(2) to (4) and Article 16(4) read with the Directive Principles of State Policy and various international instruments to which Indian is a party, call for social equality, which the TGs could realize, only if facilities and opportunities are extended to them so that they can also live with dignity and equal status with other genders.

Article 19(1) (a) and Transgenders

69. Article 19(1) of the Constitution guarantees certain fundamental rights, subject to the power of the State to impose restrictions from exercise of those rights. The

rights conferred by Article 19 are not available to any person who is not a citizen of India. Article 19(1) guarantees those great basic rights which are recognized and guaranteed as the natural rights inherent in the status of the citizen of a free country. Article 19(1) (a) of the Constitution states that all citizens shall have the right to freedom of speech and expression, which includes one's right to expression of his self-identified gender. Self-identified gender can be expressed through dress, words, action or behavior or any other form. No restriction can be placed on one's personal appearance or choice of dressing, subject to the restrictions contained in Article 19(2) of the Constitution.

70. We may, in this connection, refer to few judgments of the US Supreme Courts on the rights of TG's freedom of expression.

    70.1. The Supreme Court of the State of Illinois in the *City of Chicago v. Wilson et al.,* 75 III.2d 525(1978) struck down the municipal law prohibiting cross-dressing, and held as follows:

    "The notion that the State can regulate one's personal appearance, unconfined by any constitutional strictures whatsoever, is fundamentally inconsistent with "values of privacy, self-identity, autonomy and personal integrity that ..... the Constitution was designed to protect."

70.2. In *Doe v. Yunits* et al., 2000 WL33162199 (Mass. Super.), the Superior Court of Massachusetts, upheld the right of a person 67 to wear school dress that matches her gender identity as part of protected speech and expression and observed as follows: "by dressing in clothing and accessories traditionally associated with the female gender, she is expressing her identification with the gender. In addition, plaintiff's ability to express herself and her gender identity through dress is important for her health and wellbeing. Therefore, plaintiff's expression is not merely a personal preference but a necessary symbol of her identity."

71. The principles referred to above clearly indicate that the freedom of expression guaranteed under Article 19(1) (a) includes the freedom to express one's chosen gender identity through varied ways and means by way of expression, speech, mannerism, clothing etc.

72. Gender identity, therefore, lies at the core of one's personal identity, gender expression and presentation and, therefore, it will have to be protected under Article 19(1)(a) of the Constitution of India. A transgender's personality could be expressed by the transgender's behavior and presentation. State cannot prohibit, restrict or interfere with a transgender's expression of such personality, which reflects that inherent personality.

Often the State and its authorities either due to ignorance or otherwise fail to digest the innate character and identity of such persons. We, therefore, hold that values of privacy, self-identity, autonomy and personal integrity are fundamental rights guaranteed to members of the transgender community under Article 19(1)(a) of the Constitution of India and the State is bound to protect and recognize those rights.

Article 21 and the Transgenders

73. Article 21 of the Constitution of India reads as follows:

"21. Protection of life and personal liberty – No person shall be deprived of his life or personal liberty except according to procedure established by law."

Article 21 is the heart and soul of the Indian Constitution, which speaks of the rights to life and personal liberty. Right to life is one of the basic fundamental rights and not even the State has the authority to violate or take away that right. Article 21 takes all those aspects of life which go to make a person's life meaningful. Article 21 protects the dignity of human life, one's personal autonomy, one's right to privacy, etc. Right to dignity has been recognized to be an essential part of the right to life and accrues to all persons on account of being humans. In *Francis Coralie Mullin v. Administrator, Union Territory of Delhi* (1981) 1 SCC

608 (paras 7 and 8), this Court held that the right to dignity forms an essential part of our constitutional culture which seeks to ensure the full development and evolution of persons and includes "expressing oneself in diverse forms, freely moving about and mixing and comingling with fellow human beings".

74. The recognition of one's gender identity lies at the heart of the fundamental right to dignity. Gender, as already indicated, constitutes the core of one's sense of being as well as an integral part of a person's identity. Legal recognition of gender identity is, therefore, part of right to dignity and freedom guaranteed under our Constitution.

75. Article 21, as already indicated, guarantees the protection of "personal autonomy" of an individual. In *Anuj Garg v. Hotel Association of India* (2008) 3 SCC 1 (paragraphs 34-35), this Court held that personal autonomy includes both the negative right of not to be subject to interference by others and the positive right of individuals to make decisions about their life, to express themselves and to choose which activities to take part in. Self-determination of gender is an integral part of personal autonomy and self-expression and falls within the realm of personal liberty guaranteed under Article 21 of the Constitution of India.

Legal recognition of Third/Transgender Identity

76. Self-identified gender can be either male or female or a third gender. Hijras are identified as persons of third gender and are not identified either as male or female. Gender identity, as already indicated, refers to a person's internal sense of being male, female or a transgender, for example Hijras do not identify as female because of their lack of female genitalia or lack of reproductive capability. This distinction makes them separate from both male and female genders and they consider themselves neither man nor woman, but a "third gender". Hijras, therefore, belong to a distinct socio-religious and cultural group and have, therefore, to be considered as a "third gender", apart from male and female. State of Punjab has treated all TGs as male which is not legally sustainable. State of Tamil Nadu has taken lot of welfare measures to safeguard the rights of TGs, which we have to acknowledge. Few States like Kerala, Tripura, Bihar have referred TGs as "third gender or sex". Certain States recognize them as "third category". Few benefits have also been extended by certain other States. Our neighbouring countries have also upheld their fundamental rights and right to live with dignity.

77. The Supreme Court of Nepal in *Sunil Babu Pant & Ors. v. Nepal Government* (Writ Petition No.917 of 2007 decided on 21st December, 2007), spoke on the

rights of Transgenders as follows:

"the fundamental rights comprised under Part II of the Constitution are enforceable fundamental human rights guaranteed to the citizens against the State. For this reason, the fundamental rights stipulated in Part III are the rights similarly vested in the third gender people as human beings. The homosexuals and third gender people are also human beings as other men and women are, and they are the citizens of this country as well.... Thus, the people other than 'men' and 'women', including the people of 'third gender' cannot be discriminated. The State should recognize the existence of all natural persons including the people of third gender other than the men and women. And it cannot deprive the people of third gender from enjoying the fundamental rights provided by Part III of the Constitution."

78. The Supreme Court of Pakistan in *Dr. Mohammad Aslam Khaki & Anr. v. Senior Superintendent of Police (Operation) Rawalpindi & Ors.* (Constitution Petition No.43 of 2009) decided on 22nd March, 2011, had occasion to consider the rights of eunuchs and held as follows:

"Needless to observe that eunuchs in their rights are citizens of this country and subject to the

Constitution of the Islamic Republic of Pakistan, 1973, their rights, obligations including right to life and dignity are equally protected. Thus no discrimination, for any reason, is possible against them as far as their rights and obligations are concerned. The Government functionaries both at federal and provincial levels are bound to provide them protection of life and property and secure their dignity as well, as is done in case of other citizens."

79. We may remind ourselves of the historical presence of the third gender in this country as well as in the neighbouring countries.

80. Article 21, as already indicated, protects one's right of self- determination of the gender to which a person belongs. Determination of gender to which a person belongs is to be decided by the person concerned. In other words, gender identity is integral to the dignity of an individual and is at the core of "personal autonomy" and "self-determination". Hijras/Eunuchs, therefore, have to be considered as Third Gender, over and above binary genders under our Constitution and the laws.

81. Articles 14, 15, 16, 19 and 21, above discussion, would indicate, do not exclude Hijras/Transgenders from its ambit, but Indian law on the whole recognize the paradigm of binary genders of male and female, based on one's biological sex. As already indicated, we cannot

accept the Corbett principle of "Biological Test", rather we prefer to follow the psyche of the person in determining sex and gender and prefer the "Psychological Test" instead of "Biological Test". Binary notion of gender reflects in the Indian Penal Code, for example, Section 8, 10, etc. and also in the laws related to marriage, adoption, divorce, inheritance, succession and other welfare legislations like NAREGA, 2005, etc. Non-recognition of the identity of Hijras/Transgenders in the various legislations denies them equal protection of law and they face wide-spread discrimination.

82. Article 14 has used the expression "person" and the Article 15 has used the expression "citizen" and "sex" so also Article 16. Article 19 has also used the expression "citizen". Article 21 has used the expression "person". All these expressions, which are "gender neutral" evidently refer to human-beings. Hence, they take within their sweep Hijras/Transgenders and are not as such limited to male or female gender. Gender identity as already indicated forms the core of one's personal self, based on self identification, not on surgical or medical procedure. Gender identity, in our view, is an integral part of sex and no citizen can be discriminated on the ground of gender identity, including those who identify as third gender.

83. We, therefore, conclude that discrimination on the basis of sexual orientation or gender identity includes any

discrimination, exclusion, restriction or preference, which has the effect of nullifying or transposing equality by the law or the equal protection of laws guaranteed under our Constitution, and hence we are inclined to give various directions to safeguard the constitutional rights of the members of the TG community.

DR. A.K. SIKRI, J.

84. I have carefully, and with lot of interest, gone through the perspicuous opinion of my brother Radhakrishnan J. I am entirely in agreement with the discussion contained in the said judgment on all the cardinal issues that have arisen for consideration in these proceedings. At the same time, having regard to the fact that the issues involved are of seminal importance, I am also inclined to pen down my thoughts.

85. As is clear, these petitions essentially raise an issue of "Gender Identity", which is the core issue. It has two facets, viz.:

"(a) Whether a person who is born as a male with predominantly female orientation (or vice-versa), has a right to get himself to be recognized as a female as per his choice moreso, when such a person after having undergone operational procedure, changes his/her sex as well;

(b) Whether transgender (TG), who are neither

males nor females, have a right to be identified and categorized as a "third gender"?

86. We would hasten to add that it is the second issue with which we are primarily concerned in these petitions though in the process of discussion, first issue which is somewhat inter-related, has also popped up.

87. Indubitably, the issue of choice of gender identify has all the trappings of a human rights. That apart, as it becomes clear from the reading of the judgment of my esteemed Brother Radhakrishnan J., the issue is not limited to the exercise of choice of gender/sex. Many rights which flow from this choice also come into play, inasmuch not giving them the status of a third gender results in depriving the community of TGs of many of their valuable rights and privileges which other persons enjoy as citizens of this Country. There is also deprivation of social and cultural participation which results into eclipsing their access to education and health services. Radhakrishnan, J. has exhaustively described the term 'Transgender' as an umbrella term which embraces within itself a wide range of identities and experiences including but not limited to pre- operative/post-operative trans sexual people who strongly identify with the gender opposite to their biological sex i.e. male/ female. Therein, the history of transgenders in India is also traced and while doing so, there is mention of upon the draconian legislation enacted during the British Rule,

known as Criminal Tribes Act, 1871 which treated, per se, the entire community of Hizra persons as innately 'criminals', 'addicted to the systematic commission of non-bailable offences'.

88. With these introductory remarks, I revert to the two facets of pivotal importance mentioned above. Before embarking on the discussion, I may clarify that my endeavour would be not to repeat the discussion contained in the judgment of my Brother Radhakrishnan, J., as I agree with every word written therein. However, at times, if some of the observations are re-narrated, that would be only with a view to bring continuity in the thought process.

(1) Re: Right of a person to have the gender of his/her choice

89. When a child is born, at the time of birth itself, sex is assigned to him/her. A child would be treated with that sex thereafter, i.e. either a male or a female. However, as explained in detail in the accompanying judgment, some persons, though relatively very small in number, may born with bodies which incorporate both or certain aspects of both male or female physiology. It may also happen that though a person is born as a male, because of some genital anatomy problems his innate perception may be that of a female and all his actions would be female oriented. The position may be exactly the

opposite wherein a person born as female may behave like a male person.

90. In earlier times though one could observe such characteristics, at the same time the underlying rationale or reason behind such a behavior was not known. Over a period of time, with in depth study and research of such physical and psychological factors bevaviour, the causes of this behaviour have become discernable which in turn, has led to some changes in societal norms. Society has starting accepting, though slowly, these have accepted the behavioral norms of such persons without treating it as abnormal. Further, medical science has leaped forward to such an extent that even physiology appearance of a person can be changed through surgical procedures, from male to female and vice-versa. In this way, such persons are able to acquire the body which is in conformity with the perception of their gender/gender characteristics. In order to ensure that law also keeps pace with the aforesaid progress in medical science, various countries have come out with Legislation conferring rights on such persons to recognize their gender identity based on reassigned sex after undergoing Sex Re-Assignment Surgery (SRS). Law and judgments given by the courts in other countries have been exhaustively and grandiloquently traversed by my learned Brother in his judgment, discussing amongst others, the Yogyakarta principles, the relevant provisions of the Universal

Declaration of Human Rights 1948 and highlighting the statutory framework operating in those countries.

91. The genesis of this recognition lies in the acknowledgment of another fundamental and universal principal viz. "right of choice" given to an individual which is the inseparable part of human rights. It is a matter of historical significance that the 20th Century is often described as "the age of rights".

92. The most important lesson which was learnt as a result of Second World War was the realization by the Governments of various countries about the human dignity which needed to be cherished and protected. It is for this reason that in the U.N. Charter, 1945, adopted immediately after the Second World War, dignity of the individuals was mentioned as of core value. The almost contemporaneous Universal Declaration of Human Rights (1948) echoed same sentiments.

93. The underlined message in the aforesaid documents is the acknowledgment that human rights are individual and have a definite linkage of human development, both sharing common vision and with a common purpose. Respect for human rights is the root for human development and realization of full potential of each individual, which in turn leads to the augmentation of human resources with progress of the nation. Empowerment of the people through human development is the aim of human rights.

94. There is thus a universal recognition that human rights are rights that "belong" to every person, and do not depend on the specifics of the individual or the relationship between the right-holder and the right-grantor. Moreover, human rights exist irrespective of the question whether they are granted or recognized by the legal and social system within which we live. They are devices to evaluate these existing arrangements: ideally, these arrangements should not violate human rights. In other words, human rights are moral, pre-legal rights. They are not granted by people nor can they be taken away by them.

95. In international human rights law, equality is found upon two complementary principles: non-discrimination and reasonable differentiation. The principle of non-discrimination seeks to ensure that all persons can equally enjoy and exercise all their rights and freedoms. Discrimination occurs due to arbitrary denial of opportunities for equal participation. For example, when public facilities and services are set on standards out of the reach of the TGs, it leads to exclusion and denial of rights. Equality not only implies preventing discrimination (example, the protection of individuals against unfavourable treatment by introducing anti-discrimination laws), but goes beyond in remedying discrimination against groups suffering systematic discrimination in society. In concrete terms, it means

embracing the notion of positive rights, affirmative action and reasonable accommodation.

96. Nevertheless, the Universal Declaration of Human Rights recognizes that all human beings are born free and equal in dignity and rights and, since the Covenant's provisions apply fully to all members of society, persons with disabilities are clearly entitled to the full range of rights recognized in the Covenant. Moreover, the requirement contained in Article 2 of the Covenant that the rights enunciated will be exercised without discrimination of any kind based on certain specified grounds or other status clearly applies to cover persons with disabilities.

97. India attained independence within two years of adoption of the aforesaid U.N. Charter and it was but natural that such a Bill of Rights would assume prime importance insofar as thinking of the members of the Constituent Assembly goes. It in fact did and we found chapter on fundamental rights in Part-III of the Constitution. It is not necessary for me, keeping in view the topic of today's discussion, to embark on detailed discussion on Chapter-III. Some of the provisions relevant for our purposes would be Article 14, 15,16 and 21 of the Constitution which have already been adverted to in detail in the accompanying judgment. At this juncture it also needs to be emphasized simultaneously is that in addition to the fundamental

rights, Constitution makers also deemed it proper to impose certain obligations on the State in the form of "Directive Principles of State Policy" (Part-IV) as a mark of good governance. It is this part which provides an ideal and purpose to our Constitution and delineates certain principles which are fundamental in the governance of the country. Dr. Ambedkar had explained the purpose of these Directive Principles in the following manner (See Constituent Assembly debates):

"The Directive Principles are like the Instruments of Instructions which were issued to the Governor-General and the Governors of Colonies, and to those of India by the British Government under the 1935 Government of India Act. What is called "Directive Principles" is merely another name for the Instrument of Instructions. The only difference is that they are instructions to the legislature and the executive. Whoever capture power will not be free to do what he likes with it. In the exercise of it he will have to respect these instruments of instructions which are called Directive Principles".

98. The basic spirit of our Constitution is to provide each and every person of the nation equal opportunity to grow as a human being, irrespective of race, caste, religion, community and social status. Granville Austin while analyzing the functioning of Indian Constitution in first 50 years has described three distinguished strands of

Indian Constitution: (i)protecting national unity and integrity, (ii)establishing the institution and spirit of democracy; and (iii) fostering social reforms. The Strands are mutually dependent, and inextricably intertwined in what he elegantly describes as "a seamless web". And there cannot be social reforms till it is ensured that each and every citizen of this country is able to exploit his/her potentials to the maximum. The Constitution, although drafted by the Constituent Assembly, was meant for the people of India and that is why it is given by the people to themselves as expressed in the opening words "We the People". What is the most important gift to the common person given by this Constitution is "fundamental rights" which may be called Human Rights as well.

99. The concept of equality in Article 14 so also the meaning of the words 'life', 'liberty' and 'law' in Article 21 have been considerably enlarged by judicial decisions. Anything which is not 'reasonable, just and fair' is not treated to be equal and is, therefore, violative of Article 14.

100. Speaking for the vision of our founding fathers, in *State of Karnataka v. Rangnatha Reddy* (AIR 1978 SC 215), this Court speaking through Justice Krishna Iyer observed:

"The social philosophy of the Constitution shapes creative judicial vision and orientation. Our nation has, as its dynamic doctrine, economic democracy sans which political democracy is chimerical. We say so because our Constitution, in Parts III and IV and elsewhere, ensouls such a value system, and the debate in this case puts precisely this soul in peril....Our thesis is that the dialectics of social justice should not be missed if the synthesis of Parts III and Part IV is to influence State action and court pronouncements. Constitutional problems cannot be studied in a socio-economic vacuum, since socio-cultural changes are the source of the new values, and sloughing off old legal thought is part of the process the new equity- loaded legality. A judge is a social scientist in his role as constitutional invigilator and fails functionally if he forgets this dimension in his complex duties."

101. While interpreting Art. 21, this Court has comprehended such diverse aspects as children in jail entitled to special treatment (*Sheela Barse vs. Union of India* [(1986)3 SCC 596], health hazard due to pollution (*Mehta M.C. v. Union of India* [(1987) 4 SCC 463], beggars interest in housing (*Kalidas v. State of J&K* [(1987) 3 SCC 430] health hazard from harmful drugs (Vincent *Panikurlangara Vs. Union of India* AIR 1987 SC 990), right of speedy trial (*Raghubir Singh Vs. State of Bihar*, AIR 1987 SC 149), handcuffing of prisoners(*Altemesh Rein Vs. Union of India*, AIR 1988

SC 1768), delay in execution of death sentence, immediate medical aid to injured persons(Parmanand Katara Vs. Union of India, AIR 1989 SC 2039), starvation deaths(Kishen Vs. State of Orissa, AIR 1989 SC 677), the right to know(Reliance Petrochemicals Ltd. Vs. Indian Express Newspapers Bombay Pvt. Ltd. AIR 1989 SC 190), right to open trial(Kehar Singh Vs. State (Delhi Admn.) AIR 1988 SC 1883), inhuman conditions an after-care home(Vikram Deo Singh Tomar Vs. State of Bihar, AIR 1988 SC 1782).

102. A most remarkable feature of this expansion of Art.21 is that many of the non-justiciable Directive Principles embodied in Part IV of the Constitution have now been resurrected as enforceable fundamental rights by the magic wand of judicial activism, playing on Art.21 e.g.

   (a) Right to pollution-free water and air (Subhash Kumar Vs. State of Bihar, AIR 1991 SC 420).

   (b) Right to a reasonable residence (Shantistar Builders Vs. Narayan Khimalal Totame AIR 1990 SC 630).

   (c) Right to food (Supra note 14), clothing, decent environment (supra note 20) and even protection of cultural heritage (Ram Sharan Autyanuprasi Vs. UOI, AIR 1989 SC 549) .

   (d) Right of every child to a full development (Shantistar Builders v. Narayan Khimalal Totame AIR 1990 SC 630).

(e) Right of residents of hilly-areas to access to roads(State of H.P. v. Umed Ram Sharma, AIR 1986 SC 847).

(f) Right to education (Mohini Jain v. State of Karnataka, AIR 1992 SC 1858), but not for a professional degree (Unni Krishnan J.P. v. State of A.P., AIR 1993 SC 2178).

103. A corollary of this development is that while so long the negative language of Art.21 and use of the word 'deprived' was supposed to impose upon the State the negative duty not to interfere with the life or liberty of an individual without the sanction of law, the width and amplitude of this provision has now imposed a positive obligation (Vincent Panikurlangara v. Union of India, AIR 1987 SC 990) upon the State to take steps for ensuring to the individual a better enjoyment of his life and dignity, e.g.

(i) Maintenance and improvement of public health (Vincent Panikurlangara v. Union of India, AIR 1987 SC 990).

(ii) Elimination of water and air pollution (Mehta M.C. v. Union of India, (1987) 4 SCC 463).

(iii) Improvement of means of communication (State of H.P. v. Umed Ram Sharma, AIR 1986 SC 847).

(iv) Rehabilitation of bonded labourers (Bandhuva Mukti Morcha Vs. UOI, AIR 1984 SC 802).

(v) Providing human conditions if prisons (Sher Singh Vs. State of Punjab AIR 1983 SC 465) and protective homes (Sheela Barse Vs. UOI (1986) 3 SCC 596).

(vi) Providing hygienic condition in a slaughter-house (Buffalo Traders Welfare Ass. Vs. Maneka Gandhi (1994) Suppl (3) SCC 448).

104. The common golden thread which passes through all these pronouncements is that Art.21 guarantees enjoyment of life by all citizens of this country with dignity, viewing this human rights in terms of human development.

105. The concepts of justice social, economic and political, equality of status and of opportunity and of assuring dignity of the individual incorporated in the Preamble, clearly recognize the right of one and all amongst the citizens of these basic essentials designed to flower the citizen's personality to its fullest. The concept of equality helps the citizens in reaching their highest potential.

106. Thus, the emphasis is on the development of an individual in all respects. The basic principle of the dignity and freedom of the individual is common to all nations, particularly those having democratic set up. Democracy requires us to respect and develop the free spirit of human being which is responsible for all progress in human history. Democracy is also a method by which we attempt to raise the living standard of the

people and to give opportunities to every person to develop his/her personality. It is founded on peaceful co-existence and cooperative living. If democracy is based on the recognition of the individuality and dignity of man, as a fortiori we have to recognize the right of a human being to choose his sex/gender identity which is integral his/her personality and is one of the most basic aspect of self-determination dignity and freedom. In fact, there is a growing recognition that the true measure of development of a nation is not economic growth; it is human dignity.

107. More than 225 years ago, Immanuel Kant propounded the doctrine of free will, namely the free willing individual as a natural law ideal. Without going into the detail analysis of his aforesaid theory of justice (as we are not concerned with the analysis of his jurisprudence) what we want to point out is his emphasis on the "freedom" of human volition. The concepts of volition and freedom are "pure" that is not drawn from experience. They are independent of any particular body of moral or legal rules. They are presuppositions of all such rules, valid and necessary for all of them.

108. Over a period of time, two divergent interpretations of the Kantian criterion of justice came to be discussed. One trend was an increasing stress on the maximum of individual freedom of action as the end of law. This may not be accepted and was criticized by the protagonist of

'hedonist utilitarianism', notably Bentham. This school of thoughts laid emphasis on the welfare of the society rather than an individual by propounding the principle of maximum of happiness to most of the people. Fortunately, in the instant case, there is no such dichotomy between the individual freedom/liberty we are discussing, as against public good. On the contrary, granting the right to choose gender leads to public good. The second tendency of Kantian criterion of justice was found in re-interpreting "freedom" in terms not merely of absence of restraint but in terms of attainment of individual perfection. It is this latter trend with which we are concerned in the present case and this holds good even today. As pointed out above, after the Second World War, in the form of U.N. Charter and thereafter there is more emphasis on the attainment of individual perfection. In that united sense at least there is a revival of natural law theory of justice. Blackstone, in the opening pages in his 'Vattelian Fashion' said that the principal aim of society "is to protect individuals in the enjoyment of those absolute rights which were vested in them by the immutable laws of nature......"

109. In fact, the recognition that every individual has fundamental right to achieve the fullest potential, is founded on the principle that all round growth of an individual leads to common public good. After all, human beings are also valuable asset of any country who

contribute to the growth and welfare of their nation and the society. A person who is born with a particular sex and his forced to grow up identifying with that sex and not a sex that his/her psychological behavior identifies with, faces innumerable obstacles in growing up. In an article appeared in the magazine "Eye" of the Sunday Indian Express (March 9-15, 2014) a person born as a boy but with trappings of female (who is now a female after SRS) has narrated these difficulties in the following manner:

"The other children treated me as a boy, but I preferred playing with girls. Unfortunately, grown-ups consider that okay only as long as you are a small child. The constant inner conflict made things difficult for me and, as I grew up, I began to dread social interactions".

Such a person, carrying dual entity simultaneously, would encounter mental and psychological difficulties which would hinder his/her normal mental and even physical growth. It is not even easy for such a person to take a decision to undergo SRS procedure which requires strong mental state of affairs. However, once that is decided and the sex is changed in tune with psychological behavior, it facilitates spending the life smoothly. Even the process of transition is not smooth. The transition from a man to a woman is not an overnight process. It is a "painfully" long procedure that requires a lot of patience. A person must first undergo hormone therapy and, if possible, live as a member of the desired sex for a while. To be eligible for hormone therapy, the person needs at least two psychiatrists to certify that he or she is mentally sound, and schizophrenia, depression and transvestism have to be ruled out first. The psychiatric evaluation involved a serious a questions on how Sunaina felt, when she got to know of her confusion and need for sex change, whether she is a recluse, her socio-economic condition, among other things.

110. In the same article appearing in the "Eye" referred to above, the person who had undergone the operation and became a complete girl, Sunaina (name changed) narrates the benefit which ensued because of change in sex, in harmony with her emotional and psychological character, as is clear from the following passage in that article:

"Like many other single people in the city, she can spend hours watching Friends, and reading thrillers and Harry Potter. A new happiness has taken seed in her and she says it does not feel that she ever had a male body. "I am a person who likes to laugh. Till my surgery, behind every smile of mine, there was a struggle. Now it's about time that I laughed for real. I have never had a relationship in my life, because somewhere, I always wanted to be treated as a girl. Now, that I am a woman, I am open to a new life, new relationships. I don't have to hide anymore, I don't feel trapped anymore. I love coding and my job. I love cooking. I am learning French and when my left foot recovers fully, I plan to learn dancing. And, for the first time this year, I will vote with my new name. I am looking forward to that," she says.

111. If a person has changed his/her sex in tune with his/her gender characteristics and perception, which has become possible because of the advancement in medical science, and when that is permitted by in medical ethics with no legal embargo, we do not find any impediment, legal or otherwise, in giving due recognition to the gender identity based on the reassign sex after undergoing SRS.

112. For these reasons, we are of the opinion that even in the absence of any statutory regime in this country, a person has a constitutional right to get the recognition as male or female after SRS, which was not only his/her gender characteristic but has become his/her physical form as well.

(2) Re: Right of TG to be identified and categorized as "third gender".

113. At the outset, it may be clarified that the term 'transgender' is used in a wider sense, in the present age. Even Gay, Lesbian, bisexual are included by the descriptor 'transgender'. Etymologically, the term

'transgender' is derived from two words, namely 'trans' and 'gender'. Former is a Latin word which means 'across' or 'beyond'. The grammatical meaning of 'transgender', therefore, is across or beyond gender. This has come to be known as umbrella term which includes Gay men, Lesbians, bisexuals, and cross dressers within its scope. However, while dealing with the present issue we are not concerned with this aforesaid wider meaning of the expression transgender.

114. It is to be emphasized that Transgender in India have assumed distinct and separate class/category which is not prevalent in other parts of the World except in some neighbouring countries. In this country, TG community comprise of Hijaras, enunch, Kothis, Aravanis, Jogappas, Shiv- Shakthis etc. In Indian community transgender are referred as Hizra or the third gendered people. There exists wide range of transgender-related identities, cultures, or experience –including Hijras, Aravanis, Kothis, jogtas/Jogappas, and Shiv-Shakthis (Hijras: They are biological males who reject their masculinity identity in due course of time to identify either as women, or 'not men'. Aravanis: Hijras in Tamil Nadu identify as 'Aravani'. Kothi: Kothis are heterogeneous group. Kothis can be described as biological males who show varying degrees of 'feminity'. Jogtas/Jogappas: They are those who are dedicated to serve as servant of Goddess Renukha Devi whose temples are present in Maharashtra

and Karnataka. Sometimes, Jogti Hijras are used to denote such male-to-female transgender persons who are devotees of Goddess Renukha and are also from the Hijra community. Shiv-Shakthis: They are considered as males who are possessed by or particularly close to a goddess and who have feminine gender expression). The way they behave and acts differs from the normative gender role of a men and women. For them, furthering life is far more difficult since such people are neither categorized as men nor women and this deviation is unacceptable to society's vast majority. Endeavour to live a life with dignity is even worse. Obviously transvestites, the hijra beg from merchants who quickly, under threat of obscene abuse, respond to the silent demands of such detested individuals. On occasion, especially festival days, they press their claims with boisterous and ribald singing and dancing.(A Right to Exist: Eunuchs and the State in Nineteenth-Century India Laurence W. Preston Modern Asian Studies, Vol.21,No.2 (1987), pp.371-387).

115. Therefore, we make it clear at the outset that when we discuss about the question of conferring distinct identity, we are restrictive in our meaning which has to be given to TG community i.e. hijra etc., as explained above.

116. Their historical background and individual scenario has been stated in detail in the accompanying judgment rendered by my learned Brother. Few things which

follow from this discussion are summed up below:

116.1 Though in the past TG in India was treated with great respect that does not remain the scenario any longer. Attrition in their status was triggered with the passing of the Criminal Tribes Act, 1871 which deemed the entire community of Hijara persons as innately 'criminal' and 'adapted to the systematic commission of non-bailable offences'. This dogmatism and indoctrination of Indian people with aforesaid presumption, was totally capricious and nefarious. There could not have been more harm caused to this community with the passing of the aforesaid brutal Legislation during British Regime with the vicious and savage this mind set. To add insult to the irreparable injury caused, Section 377 of the Indian Penal Code was misused and abused as there was a tendency, in British period, to arrest and prosecute TG persons under Section 377 merely on suspicion. To undergo this sordid historical harm caused to TGs of India, there is a need for incessant efforts with effervescence.

116.2 There may have been marginal improvement in the social and economic condition of TGs in India. It is still far from satisfactory and these TGs continue to face different kinds of economic blockade and social degradation. They still face multiple forms of oppression in this country. Discrimination qua them is clearly discernable in various fields including health care, employment, education, social cohesion etc.

116.3 The TGs are also citizens of this country. They also have equal right to achieve their full potential as human beings. For this purpose, not only they are entitled to proper education, social assimilation, access to public and other places but employment opportunities as well. The discussion above while dealing with the first issue, therefore, equally applies to this issue as well.

117. We are of the firm opinion that by recognizing such TGs as third gender, they would be able to enjoy their human rights, to which they are largely deprived of for want of this recognition. As mentioned above, the issue of transgender is not merely a social or medical issue but there is a need to adopt human right approach towards transgenders which may focus on functioning as an interaction between a person and their environment highlighting the role of society and changing the stigma attached to them. TGs face many disadvantages due to various reasons, particularly for gender abnormality which in certain level needs to physical and mental disability. Up till recently they were subjected to cruelty, pity or charity. Fortunately, there is a paradigm shift in thinking from the aforesaid approach to a rights based approach. Though, this may be the thinking of human rights activist, the society has not kept pace with this shift. There appears to be limited public knowledge and understanding of same-sex sexual orientation and people whose gender identity and expression are incongruent with their biological sex. As a result of this approach, such persons are socially excluded from the mainstream of the society and they are denied equal access to those fundamental rights and freedoms that the other people enjoy freely.(See, Hijras/Transgender Women in India: HIV, Human Rights and Social Exclusion, UNDP report on India Issue: December, 2010).

118. Some of the common and reported problem that transgender most commonly suffer are: harassment by the police in public places, harassment at home, police entrapment, rape, discriminations, abuse in public places et.al. The other major problems that the transgender people face in their daily life are discrimination, lack of educational facilities, lack of medical facilities, homelessness, unemployment, depression, hormone pill abuse, tobacco and alcohol abuse, and problems related to marriage and adoption. In spite of the adoption of Universal Declaration of Human Rights (UDHR) in the year 1948, the inherent dignity, equality, respect and rights of all human beings throughout the world, the transgender are denied basic human rights. This denial is premised on a prevalent juridical assumption that the

law should target discrimination based on sex (i.e., whether a person is anatomically male or female), rather than gender (i.e., whether a person has qualities that society consider masculine or feminine (Katherine M.Franke, The Central Mistake of Sex Discrimination Law: the Disaggregation of Sex from Gender, 144 U.Pa.Rev.1,3 (1995) (arguing that by defining sex in biological terms, the law has failed to distinguish sex from gender, and sexual differentiation from sex discrimination). Transgender people are generally excluded from the society and people think transgenderism as a medical disease. Much like the disability, which in earlier times was considered as an illness but later on looked upon as a right based approach. The question whether transgenderism is a disease is hotly debated in both the transgender and medical-psychiatric communities. But a prevalent view regarding this is that transgenderism is not a disease at all, but a benign normal variant of the human experience akin to left- handedness.

119. Therefore, gender identification becomes very essential component which is required for enjoying civil rights by this community. It is only with this recognition that many rights attached to the sexual recognition as 'third gender' would be available to this community more meaningfully viz. the right to vote, the right to own property, the right to marry, the right to claim a formal

identity through a passport and a ration card, a driver's license, the right to education, employment, health so on.

120. Further, there seems to be no reason why a transgender must be denied of basic human rights which includes Right to life and liberty with dignity, Right to Privacy and freedom of expression, Right to Education and Empowerment, Right against violence, Right against Exploitation and Right against Discrimination. Constitution has fulfilled its duty of providing rights to transgenders. Now it's time for us to recognize this and to extend and interpret the Constitution in such a manner to ensure a dignified life of transgender people. All this can be achieved if the beginning is made with the recognition that TG as third gender.

121. In order to translate the aforesaid rights of TGs into reality, it becomes imperative to first assign them their proper 'sex'. As is stated earlier, at the time of birth of a child itself, sex is assigned. However, it is either male or female. In the process, the society as well as law, has completely ignored the basic human right of TGs to give them their appropriate sex categorization. Up to now, they have either been treated as male or female. This is not only improper as it is far from truth, but indignified to these TGs and violates their human rights.

122. Though there may not be any statutory regime recognizing 'third gender' for these TGs. However, we

find enough justification to recognize this right of theirs in natural law sphere. Further, such a justification can be traced to the various provisions contained in Part III of the Constitution relating to 'Fundamental Rights'. In addition to the powerful justification accomplished in the accompanying opinion of my esteemed Brother, additional raison d'etre for this conclusion is stated hereinafter.

123. We are in the age of democracy, that too substantive and liberal democracy. Such a democracy is not based solely on the rule of people through their representatives' namely formal democracy. It also has other percepts like Rule of Law, human rights, independence of judiciary, separation of powers etc.

124. There is recognition to the hard realty that without protection for human rights there can be no democracy and no justification for democracy. In this scenario, while working within the realm of separation of powers (which is also fundamental to the substantive democracy), the judicial role is not only to decide the dispute before the Court, but to uphold the rule of law and ensure access to justice to the marginalized section of the society. It cannot be denied that TGs belong to the unprivileged class which is a marginalized section.

125. The role of the Court is to understand the central purpose and theme of the Constitution for the welfare of the society. Our Constitution, like the law of the

society, is a living organism. It is based on a factual and social realty that is constantly changing. Sometimes a change in the law precedes societal change and is even intended to stimulate it. Sometimes, a change in the law is the result in the social realty. When we discuss about the rights of TGs in the constitutional context, we find that in order to bring about complete paradigm shift, law has to play more pre-dominant role. As TGs in India, are neither male nor female, treating them as belonging to either of the aforesaid categories, is the denial of these constitutional rights. It is the denial of social justice which in turn has the effect of denying political and economic justice.

126. In *Dattatraya Govind Mahajan vs. State of Maharashtra* (AIR 1977 SC 915) this Court observed:

"Our Constitution is a tryst with destiny, preamble with luscent solemnity in the words 'Justice – social, economic and political.' The three great branches of Government, as creatures of the Constitution, must remember this promise in their fundamental role and forget it at their peril, for to do so will be a betrayal of chose high values and goals which this nation set for itself in its objective Resolution and whose elaborate summation appears in Part IV of the Paramount Parchment. The history of our country's struggle for independence was the story of a battle between the forces of socio-economic exploitation and the masses of deprived people of varying degrees and the Constitution sets the new sights of the nation......Once we grasp the dharma of the Constitution, the new orientation of the karma of adjudication becomes clear. Our founding fathers, aware of our social realities, forged our fighting faith and integrating justice in its social, economic and political aspects. While contemplating the meaning of the Articles of the Organic Law, the Supreme Court shall not disown Social Justice."

127. Oliver Wendlle Holmes said: "the life of law has been logical; it has been experience". It may be added that 'the life of law is not just logic or experience. The life of law is renewable based on experience and logic, which adapted law to the new social realty'. Recognizing this fact, the aforesaid provisions of the Constitution are required to be given new and dynamic meaning with the inclusion of rights of TGs as well. In this process, the first and foremost right is to recognize TGs as 'third gender' in law as well. This is recognition of their right of equality enshrined in Art.14 as well as their human right to life with dignity, which is the mandate of the Art.21 of the Constitution. This interpretation is in consonance with new social needs. By doing so, this Court is only bridging the gap between the law and life and that is the primary role of the Court in a democracy. It only amounts to giving purposive interpretation to

the aforesaid provisions of the Constitution so that it can adapt to the changes in realty. Law without purpose has no raison d'etre. The purpose of law is the evolution of a happy society. As Justice Iyer has aptly put:

"The purpose of law is the establishment of the welfare of society "and a society whose members enjoy welfare and happiness may be described as a just society. It is a negation of justice to say that some members, some groups, some minorities, some individuals do not have welfare: on the other hand they suffer from ill-fare. So it is axiomatic that law, if it is to fulfil itself, must produce a contented, dynamic society which is at once meting out justice to its members."

128. It is now very well recognized that the Constitution is a living character; its interpretation must be dynamic. It must be understood in a way that intricate and advances modern realty. The judiciary is the guardian of the Constitution and by ensuring to grant legitimate right that is due to TGs, we are simply protecting the Constitution and the democracy inasmuch as judicial protection and democracy in general and of human rights in particular is a characteristic of our vibrant democracy.

129. As we have pointed out above, our Constitution inheres liberal and substantive democracy with rule of law as an important and fundamental pillar. It has its own internal

morality based on dignity and equality of all human beings. Rule of law demands protection of individual human rights. Such rights are to be guaranteed to each and every human being. These TGs, even though insignificant in numbers, are still human beings and therefore they have every right to enjoy their human rights.

130. In National Human Rights Commission v. State of Arunachal Pradesh (AIR 1996 SC 1234), This Court observed:

"We are a country governed by the Rule of Law. Our Constitution confers certain rights on every human being and certain other rights on citizens. Every person is entitled to equality before the law and equal protection of the laws."

131. The rule of law is not merely public order. The rule of law is social justice based on public order. The law exists to ensure proper social life. Social life, however, is not a goal in itself but a means to allow the individual to life in dignity and development himself. The human being and human rights underlie this substantive perception of the rule of law, with a proper balance among the different rights and between human rights and the proper needs of society. The substantive rule of law "is the rule of proper law, which balances the needs of society and the individual." This is the rule of law that strikes a balance between society's need for political

independence, social equality, economic development, and internal order, on the one hand, and the needs of the individual, his personal liberty, and his human dignity on the other. It is the duty of the Court to protect this rich concept of the rule of law.

132. By recognizing TGs as third gender, this Court is not only upholding the rule of law but also advancing justice to the class, so far deprived of their legitimate natural and constitutional rights. It is, therefore, the only just solution which ensures justice not only to TGs but also justice to the society as well. Social justice does not mean equality before law in papers but to translate the spirit of the Constitution, enshrined in the Preamble, the Fundamental Rights and the Directive Principles of State Policy into action, whose arms are long enough to bring within its reach and embrace this right of recognition to the TGs which legitimately belongs to them.

133. Aristotle opined that treating all equal things equal and all unequal things unequal amounts to justice. Kant was of the view that at the basis of all conceptions of justice, no matter which culture or religion has inspired them, lies the golden rule that you should treat others as you would want everybody to treat everybody else, including yourself. When Locke conceived of individual liberties, the individuals he had in mind were independently rich males. Similarly, Kant thought of economically self-sufficient males as the only possible citizens of a liberal

democratic state. These theories may not be relevant in today's context as it is perceived that the bias of their perspective is all too obvious to us. In post-traditional liberal democratic theories of justice, the background assumption is that humans have equal value and should, therefore, be treated as equal, as well as by equal laws. This can be described as 'Reflective Equilibrium'. The method of Reflective Equilibrium was first introduced by Nelson Goodman in 'Fact, Fiction and Forecast' (1955). However, it is John Rawls who elaborated this method of Reflective Equilibrium by introducing the conception of 'Justice as Fairness'. In his 'Theory of Justice', Rawls has proposed a model of just institutions for democratic societies. Herein he draws on certain pre-theoretical elementary moral beliefs ('considered judgments'), which he assumes most members of democratic societies would accept. "[Justice as fairness [....] tries to draw solely upon basic intuitive ideas that are embedded in the political institutions of a constitutional democratic regime and the public traditions of their interpretations. Justice as fairness is a political conception in part because it starts from within a certain political tradition. Based on this preliminary understanding of just institutions in a democratic society, Rawls aims at a set of universalistic rules with the help of which the justice of present formal and informal institutions can be assessed. The ensuing conception of justice is called 'justice as fairness'. When we combine Rawls's notion of Justice as Fairness with the notions of Distributive Justice, to which Noble Laureate Professor Amartya Sen has also subscribed, we get jurisprudential basis for doing justice to the Vulnerable Groups which definitely include TGs. Once it is accepted that the TGs are also part of vulnerable groups and marginalized section of the society, we are only bringing them within the fold of aforesaid rights recognized in respect of other classes falling in the marginalized group. This is the minimum riposte in an attempt to assuage the insult and injury suffered by them so far as to pave way for fast tracking the realization of their human rights.

134. The aforesaid, thus, are my reasons for treating TGs as 'third gender' for the purposes of safeguarding and enforcing appropriately their rights guaranteed under the Constitution. These are my reasons in support of our Constitution to the two issues in these petitions.

135. We, therefore, declare:

(1) Hijras, Eunuchs, apart from binary gender, be treated as "third gender" for the purpose of safeguarding their rights under Part III of our Constitution and the laws made by the Parliament and the State Legislature.

(2) Transgender persons' right to decide their self-identified gender is also upheld and the Centre and

State Governments are directed to grant legal recognition of their gender identity such as male, female or as third gender.

(3) We direct the Centre and the State Governments to take steps to treat them as socially and educationally backward classes of citizens and extend all kinds of reservation in cases of admission in educational institutions and for public appointments. (4) Centre and State Governments are directed to operate separate HIV Sero-survellance Centres since Hijras/ Transgenders face several sexual health issues.

(5) Centre and State Governments should seriously address the problems being faced by Hijras/ Transgenders such as fear, shame, gender dysphoria, social pressure, depression, suicidal tendencies, social stigma, etc. and any insistence for SRS for declaring one's gender is immoral and illegal.

(6) Centre and State Governments should take proper measures to provide medical care to TGs in the hospitals and also provide them separate public toilets and other facilities.

(7) Centre and State Governments should also take steps for framing various social welfare schemes for their betterment.

(8) Centre and State Governments should take steps

to create public awareness so that TGs will feel that they are also part and parcel of the social life and be not treated as untouchables.

(9) Centre and the State Governments should also take measures to regain their respect and place in the society which once they enjoyed in our cultural and social life.

136. We are informed an Expert Committee has already been constituted to make an in-depth study of the problems faced by the Transgender community and suggest measures that can be taken by the Government to ameliorate their problems and to submit its report with recommendations within three months of its constitution. Let the recommendations be examined based on the legal declaration made in this Judgment and implemented within six months.

137. Writ Petitions are, accordingly, allowed, as above.

Appreciation of the Judgment by National as well as International Media

1. ENDING THE GENDER BINARY[1]

Chapal Mehra

In this election din, between empty slogans and personal slandering, has come one of India's proudest moments as a nation — one that values equality, justice and freedom of even its most marginalised. On April 15, 2014, the Supreme Court gave a landmark judgment granting India's transgender community the right to be recognised as a third gender category. Additionally, it ruled that it was every human being's right to choose one's own gender.

Challenging the Dominant View

With this judgment, the Court has challenged the dominant view of gender identity. In a society that has focused on a binary, this is revolutionary. In this judgment, the court recognises that "individual experience" of gender is one of the most fundamental aspects of "self-determination, dignity and freedom." Further the judgment relates the right to freedom of expression to one's right to express one's self-identified gender. Thus, the idea of gender is transformed from social acceptability to individual choice and experience.

The judgment is significant in many other ways as well. By ending the gender binary, the Court has opened the discussion on the rights of marriage, adoption and inheritance for the

---

[1] The Hindu, April 22, 2014.

transgender community. The judgment also recognizes the community's position as a socially and economically backward category, and directs the state for appropriate affirmative action. More specifically, it directs the state to provide the community access to health services and even separate toilets.

For India's transgender community, it is their first encounter with equality in a democratic framework. At the same time, this thoughtful, inclusive judgment is significant for all Indians, especially minorities. It comes at a time when India's political parties are engaged in a vitriolic confrontation over minorities and their rights. The Court's interpretation — of justice, equality, freedom and dignity and the role of the state — should remind our political class that the rights of Indian citizens, irrespective of gender or sexual orientation, are safeguarded by the Constitution. The judges quote Aristotle, Kant, Rawls and Amartya Sen to create a broader narrative on justice — something extremely relevant to this election.

Despite the euphoria, the judgment is not without problems. A broad sweep of identities neglects many identities. Also, the procedures for implementation lie with the States and the Centre. Interestingly, it also evades extensive comment on Section 377 which criminalizes sex between homosexuals, which the judges term as a "colonial legacy." It remains to be seen how this judgment will interact with the petition on Section 377, to be considered soon. Rationally, it will be difficult to give citizens the right to choose their gender but not the right to choose who they love. The Court's decision on Section 377 will tell us whether the highest court in the land can live with deeply contradictory ideas of justice, freedom, and equality.

Yet, the process of change will now be irreversible. Just as law can manufacture intolerance, it can also create gradual social acceptance. Social attitudes may not transform overnight but Indian society only needs to look at its own history of inclusiveness. The transgender community was, until the advent of colonialism, a respected section of society. The Hindu Right should note that transgenders are mentioned in the Ramayana, and that it is Ram who gives them the power to bless important occasions such as childbirth and marriage. Also, Shiva's Ardhanarishwar form is well-known and widely worshipped.

The Role of the British

The tradition is not limited to Hinduism alone. Islamic, Jain and other cultures have also included the transgender community and other sexual minorities. The famous Sufi saint, Bulle Shah, dressed as a woman to please his master and often danced with eunuchs. Yet all this changed when India was colonized. The Indian Penal Code enacted by the British recognised only two genders, creating a binary that never existed.

Over time, these constructs were absorbed in Indian society. The community has since faced extreme forms of violence for not conforming to socially dictated gender identities. This violence often happens within families and communities, where transgenders face abuse, discrimination, disinheritance and abandonment. This judgment will hopefully begin to alter this in some measure.

Despite its many flaws and the incremental nature of this change, this is a moment of celebration not just for India's transgender community or its sexual minorities but for all minorities. In a deeply fractured democracy, the Court has safeguarded the right to individual choice and freedom. It is reassuring for every Indian that despite our debasing politics, justice, equality and individual liberty — ideas that define India — will be safeguarded, and the right to choose our identity will go beyond the binary.

2. TRANSGENDER RIGHTS IN INDIA[2]

In mid-April, India's Supreme Court recognized transgender people as a legal third gender. Grounding its decision on rights guaranteed by the nation's Constitution as well as international law, the court determined gender identity and sexual orientation to be fundamental to the rights to self-determination, dignity and freedom.

This decision is particularly welcome after another group of justices in December reinstated a colonial-era law that bans gay sex: Section 377 of the Indian Penal Code, which bars "carnal intercourse against the order of nature." The two contradictory decisions — issued by separate panels of judges — are the result of a quirk of the system. The Supreme Court consists of a chief justice and 30 other justices, with cases often being decided by panels of just two or three judges.

In the transgender case, Section 377 was cited as an instrument of discrimination against transgender people. The court properly recognized the historical and diverse presence of transgender people in Indian society, referring to ancient Hindu and Jain texts and to the place of transgender people in India's Mughal courts. It listed the different traditional categories of transgender people in India, including hijras, Aravanis, Kothis, Jogtas and Shiv-Shakthis. The court was wise to make this

---

[2] By the Editorial Board, The New York Times, April 25, 2014.

point, since anti-gay-rights groups in India have tried to paint the decriminalization of gay sex and transgender identities as degenerate Western ideas alien to India's cultural traditions.

The court has directed national and state governments to redress entrenched discrimination suffered by transgender people by recognizing them as an official minority, according them quotas for public jobs and admission to educational institutions, and making sure they are not discriminated against when seeking medical care. Official identity documents are now to include a third gender box.

On Tuesday, the court also agreed to hear oral arguments for a petition challenging the December ruling that leaves Section 377 in force. As Justices K.S. Radhakrishnan and A.K. Sikri of the Supreme Court, argued in their opinion in the transgender case: Self-determined gender identity and sexual orientation are central to human rights. It is time to abolish Section 377.

3. SALUTARY JUDGMENT[3]

By recognising the transgender community as a third gender entitled to the same rights and constitutional protection as all other citizens, the Supreme Court has put in place a sound basis to end discrimination based on gender, especially gender as presumed to be assigned to individuals at birth. Further, beyond prohibiting discrimination and harassment, the Court has extended global principles of dignity, freedom and autonomy to this unfairly marginalised and vulnerable community. The verdict lays down a comprehensive framework that takes into its fold not merely the negative right against discrimination, but also "the positive right to make decisions about their lives, to express themselves and to choose which activities to take part in." In particular, its direction that they should be treated as 'socially and educationally backward' and given reservation in education and employment, is a far-reaching contribution to their all-round development. The jurisprudential basis for the judgment is that sex identity cannot be based on a mere biological test but must take into account the individual's psyche. The Court has noted that Indian law treats gender as a binary male/female concept, with sections of the Indian Penal Code and Acts related to marriage, adoption, divorce, succession, and even welfare legislation, being examples. The Court has also

---

[3] Editorial, The Hindu, April 17, 2014.

relied on the Yogyakarta Principles — norms on sexual orientation and gender identity evolved in 2006 at Yogyakarta in Indonesia — to bolster its reasoning.

The separate, but concurring, opinions of Justice K.S. Radhakrishnan and Justice A.K. Sikri contain some subtle criticism of the Supreme Court's earlier ruling in Suresh Kumar Koushal upholding Section 377 of IPC that criminalizes even consensual same-sex activity. While conscious that they cannot depart from the ruling of a Division Bench, both Judges have highlighted the fact that misuse of Section 377 is one of the principal forms of discrimination against the transgender community. By noting that Section 377, despite being linked to some sexual acts, also highlights certain identities, Mr. Justice Radhakrishnan sees a link between gender identity and sexual orientation, something that the *Koushal* formulation missed when it concluded that the provision criminalized the act and not any identity or orientation. The sentence that transgenders "even though insignificant in numbers… have every right to enjoy their human rights" is a fitting rebuttal to the claim in *Koushal* that because the LGBT community is a minuscule minority, it could not be held that the Section is invalid. Constitutional protection ought to be made available to a particular group regardless of its size. The verdict on the transgender community now provides one more reason why Section 377 ought to be amended to de-criminalize gay sex.

4. BEYOND MALE AND FEMALE, THE RIGHT TO HUMANITY[4]

Ratna Kapur

The Supreme Court judgment recognising the rights of transgendered persons is a landmark ruling and restores faith in the Court's ability to recognise gross injustice. The Bench comprising Justices K.S. Radhakrishnan and A.K. Sikri has also restored the image of the Court as capable of bold moves when it comes to addressing the denial of the right to be human simply on the basis of one's sexual status and conduct. The Court's progressive image was in tatters after the *Suresh Kumar Kaushal v. NAZ Foundation* ruling in December 2013 that re-criminalised gays and lesbians, and overruled the 2009 Delhi High Court's decision that Section 377 of the Indian Penal Code was not applicable to consensual sexual relations between adults.

Dynamic Decision

The ruling in *National Legal Services Authority (NLSA) v. Union Of India* has far-reaching implications. It is a courageous decision that embeds the rights of transgendered persons primarily within the right to equality in the Indian Constitution. In this sense it is a more dynamic decision than the Delhi High Court ruling regarding Section 377, which was largely based on the right to privacy. The Court held that non-recognition of

---

[4] The Hindu, April 19, 2014.

gender identity violates the rights to equality and life, and that transgendered persons should not be compelled to declare themselves as either male or female. The lack of recognition of their gender identity curtails their access to education, health care and public places, and results in discrimination in the exercise of their right to vote and secure employment, driving licenses and other documentation where eligibility is contingent on declaring oneself as either male or female.

While the decision is largely based on the protection of fundamental rights, the Court also relied on a host of UN human rights provisions as well as the 2006 Yogyakarta principles, which specifically recognise the human rights of sexual minorities, and which were adopted to counter discrimination on the basis of gender identity and sexual orientation. Moreover, unlike the Bench in the Kaushal case, the judges heard with approval a host of foreign judgments relating to the rights of transgendered persons, without throwing a nationalist anti-western hissy fit.

An outstanding feature of the decision is that the judges accepted the broad definition of transgender as including persons whose gender identity, gender expression or behaviour did not conform to their biological sex, and more importantly, those who did not identify with the sex assigned to them at birth. They accepted a vast array of identities and experiences that constitute the category of transgendered persons, culturally and socially, and also accepted the fact that gender identity was not necessarily biologically determined. They referred to each person's experience of gender, which may involve a freely chosen modification of bodily appearance or functions by medical or other means. Gender identity is about self-identification. Justice Sikri went so far as to state that "even gay, lesbian, bisexual are included in the description 'transgender'" and that it was an umbrella term. The idea of male and female are not regarded as natural, but as normative categories by the Court. The NLSA decision thus recognised the social construction of not only gender but also of sex as something that is performed rather than biologically determined. This argument places this decision at the cutting edge of progressive, feminist and queer thinking on issues of gender and sexuality.

The Court further held that sex discrimination in Indian constitutional law includes discrimination on the grounds of gender identity, and rejected the view that it was limited to biological sex. It held that a binary understanding of gender denied *hijras* and transgendered persons equal protection of law and constituted the basis for widespread discrimination. The Court has clearly articulated that transgendered persons should no longer be treated with cruelty, pity or charity. There needs to be a paradigm shift towards a rights-based approach where they are accepted as fully human. As Justice Sikri stated: "It is only with this recognition that many rights attached to sexual recognition as 'third gender' would be available to this community more meaningfully viz. the right to vote, the right to own property, the right to marry, the right to claim a formal identity through a passport and a ration card, a drivers license, the right to education, employment, health and so on."

The Court also addressed the arguments regarding Section 377 but expressed no view on the Kaushal case, currently the subject matter of a curative petition. The Justices did however recognise the misuse of Section 377 to harass transgendered persons. The fact that a transgendered person may be having sex with a man also implies that homosexuals or men having sex with men or transgendered perons would also be subject to such harassment, undermining a key finding in the Kaushal decision that there was no sufficient evidence on record of police harassment.

Gaps in Kaushal Case

The NLSA judgment is a hugely significant and potentially transformative decision. It affirms that there is no place in the Constitution for a hierarchy of super-humans, lesser humans and non-humans. This decision is informed, coherent, and demonstrates a familiarity with the literature as well as acute attentiveness to counsel's arguments.

It now remains to be seen whether the obvious contradictions and gaps in the Kaushal case will be remedied by the Court in a direction that ensures that homosexuals are not only accorded the same rights as citizens as transgendered persons have been accorded, but also the right to humanity.

5. HIJRA: INDIA'S THIRD GENDER CLAIMS ITS PLACE IN LAW[5]

With their glittering saris, bright makeup and a reputation for bawdy song and dance, hijras, India's transgender minority, are hard to miss. But this week, after years of discrimination, the community has finally been granted legal visibility.

On Tuesday the Supreme Court of India ruled that transgender people would be recognised on official documents under a separate "third gender" category. The change follows similar legislation in Nepal, Pakistan and Bangladesh. This means that now, for the first time, there are quotas of government jobs and college places for hijras. The decision has been cheered by activists, who say that, despite its distinguished history, the community too often faces violence and harassment.

Shwetambera Parashar from the Humsafar Trust, an Indian NGO that campaigns for LGBT rights, says the exclusion faced by the community has been acute – from doctors refusing to examine or treat hijras, to police harrasment and discrimination keeping them locked out of mainstream employment. This week's change in the law is a "big step", she says, ensuring that discrimination can now be challenged.

Hijras, who can be eunuchs, intersex or transgender, have been part of South Asia's culture for thousands of years. Eunuchs are celebrated in sacred Hindu texts such as the Mahabharata

---

[5] Homa Khaleeli, The Guardian, 16 April, 2014.

and the Kama Sutra. They also enjoyed influential positions in the Mughal courts.

When the British came to power in India, the community's fortunes changed, with the disgusted colonists passing a law in 1897 classing all eunuchs as criminals. Since then many have been ostracized – either for cross dressing or being intersex – and have gone on to form their own communities, around a guru or mother figure to provide emotional and financial security. Many even took to using a secret code language known as Hijra Farsi for protection. More recently, hijras have been seen as auspicious and are often asked to bless celebrations such as marriages and births. In India's larger cities this has waned, forcing many to rely on begging or prostitution. The effect of this dangerous work and the community's limited access to health and welfare services can be seen in the staggering fact that HIV rates among hijras stand at 18% in Mumbai, while the rate among the wider population is only 0.3%.

Yet, despite welcoming the change in the law, Indian activists warn that not all transgender people feel comfortable being referred to as "third sex". Many prefer to be classed simply by the gender they have chosen, as women or men. Campaigners point out that more needs to be done to stop transgender people, and hijra communities in particular, from being criminalised – such as overturning the controversial section 377 law that makes homosexual acts a crime.

Bindiya Rana, who was the first transgender woman to stand as a provincial political candidate in Pakistan, says the changes in law in her own country, which came into effect in 2012, have not been enough to change lives.

"In Pakistan we are recognised and there are some jobs – mostly on three-month contracts or with NGOs – but not across the employment sector," she says. "The government have not supported us – they haven't implemented the law. I had more opposition when I fought in the election from politicians than I did from the public. Society in Pakistan is more understanding, more accepting and supportive of us than the government is. We have claimed our space in the law, but we are not protected by it."

6. INDIA'S TRANSGENDER LAW IS NO HELP TO ITS LESBIAN, GAY AND BISEXUAL COMMUNITIES[6]

In a landmark judgment by India's Supreme Court on Tuesday, transgender people were granted the status of a "third gender" category, recognising them as a socially and economically disadvantaged class. "It is the right of every human being to choose their gender," the detailed judgment stated, thus granting rights to those who self-identify as neither male nor female. The court also directed the central and state governments to take the necessary steps to allow for equal status by ensuring adequate healthcare, education and employment as well as separate public toilets and numerous other safeguards against discrimination. All identity documents such as birth certificates, passports and driver's licenses will now have a third gender box. The ruling stresses a number of times how much the transgender community has suffered historical abuse and discrimination.

While the ruling is in line with the tune of the Indian constitution, the verdict does not apply to sexuality, leaving India's lesbian, gay and bisexual communities in a state of flux. In fact, it contradicts a judgment made in December, by a different bench of the supreme court, which upheld the controversial section 377 of the Indian penal code that criminalized "sex against the order of nature", which is

---

[6] Ash Kotak, The Guardian, 17 April, 2014.

interpreted as gay sex. Only the ruling Congress party was quick off the mark to question the court ruling.

The transgender judgment quotes from several testimonies, illustrating the suffering of transgender persons and rightly acknowledging the role that section 377 played in discriminating against them. It is well accepted in the west that just as gender identity is integral to a person's self, dignity and freedom, so is a person's sexuality. The result is a constitutional dilemma – a colonial-era law is being interpreted in a contradictory manner by the highest court in India. Yet uniquely, both rulings fit in with India's super-conservative extended family-structured value system which is adhered to throughout the nation as well as the Hindu majority's religious beliefs.

In Hinduism, the Hijra community (eunuchs) – neither born male nor female, but self-identified as female – are historically believed to have the power to grant wishes and cast spells, and are often present at weddings and births. A transgender presence within Hindu psyche stems back to the essential Hindu epic text, the Mahabharata, where the male Shikhandi (but born the female Shikhandini) was vital in securing the Pandavas's necessary victory over the Kaurava in the great war of Kurukshetra.

While the Hijra are part of Indian society, they are still considered outsiders, being poor and generally working class. This makes it more acceptable for them to be ignored, thus preventing the judgment from being truly progressive. However, lesbian, gay and bisexual Indians also stem from middle- and upper-class society, and are therefore more threatening to the conservative structure and value system of society not only in India but where Indians have settled worldwide. Only last week a British-Asian man was imprisoned for murdering his Indian-born wife whom he married with the wish to unite his homosexuality and the value system of his community.

Somehow, in the extended family system practiced throughout India, gayness can be easily hidden or accepted. Marriage is often very much about duty, responsibility and honour, and outside these boundaries much is acceptable and ignored. Slowly the country is changing, however this new ruling questions the very essence of Indian society, family structure, form, and most importantly, family name and blood, as well as respect within society.

At the time of an election where the conservative, pro-Hindu BJP party, led by Narendra Modi is a strong contender to be elected prime minister, the two conflicting judgments made by the Supreme Court favouring transgender people against increasingly visible LGB people, seems to sit well with India's new future. Yet still we must remain hopeful.

7. INDIA'S SUPREME COURT RECOGNISES A THIRD GENDER [7]

The Supreme Court in India has issued a new law allowing transgender people to change their gender on official documents to reflect their gender identity. Many newspapers yesterday reported this as India officially recognising a "third gender" – because until the law was passed, transgender people had to register as either male or female. The law is actually more wide-ranging than this because it means anyone can change their gender on official documents to male, female or transgender depending on their self-identity. The term self-identity is crucial here: transgender people in India don't need to undergo any surgical or medical intervention to change their gender on official documents.

These new laws alone won't change the discrimination that many transgender people (often called hijra in India) face: many are excluded from mainstream employment and society – to the extent that some hospitals have reportedly refused to treat them – and are regularly harassed by police. It is however an important step in the right direction, because legal recognition can underpin greater social acceptance and community integration. The Supreme Court is also introducing quotas to increase the representation of transgender people in employment and education.

---

[7] Sophie McBain, New Statesman, 16 April, 2014.

So how does India now compare to other countries in terms of transgender rights? It is hard to find reliable, comprehensive data on laws protecting transgender people worldwide, but Amnesty International and the International both publish detailed reports on the situation in Europe: and they suggest that European countries have some catching up to do when it comes to establishing a legal framework to protect and recognise the rights of transgender and intersex people.

Last year, Germany became the first country in Europe to allow babies to be registered as "indeterminate sex" when they are born with characteristics of both sexes: until then (as in other European countries) parents were forced to assign a gender to their baby, a decision that is often accompanied by surgery to make the child's physical characteristics conform more closely to either male or female.

Several countries worldwide allow individuals to register as a third gender on their passport applications including New Zealand (2012), Bangladesh (2011) and Australia (2011) , while Nepal has allowed people to register as a third gender on its census since 2007 and Pakistan on identity cards since 2011. In the UK, individuals who are born intersex (around one in 2000 of the population) must be registered as male or female, and often undergo surgery as young babies to "enforce" this assigned gender.

European countries have also been too slow to allow individuals to change their gender on official documents to reflect their self-identity. In 1992 the European Court of Human Rights ruled that refusing to allow people to change their gender markers on official documentation was a violation of human rights – but still many European countries are lagging behind. The ILGA has published a summary of trans rights across 49 countries in Europe and found that in 16 countries there is no procedure for people to change their gender on official documents. In 24 countries in Europe, trans people must undergo sterilisation before their gender identity is recognised. In other countries they must first be diagnosed as suffering from a mental health disorder and in 19 countries you must be single to change your gender identity. Why should people be forced to make such stark choices?

While the legal system in many European countries fails to recognise individuals' gender identity, many transgender people are also subject to abuse and discrimination in other areas of life: 35 per cent of respondents to Amnesty International's survey of transgender rights said they had experienced violence or the threat of violence in the past five years.

The Supreme Court ruling in India is good news for the country's transgender population, and its impact could be even greater if it forces European countries to face up to some uncomfortable home truths.

8. INDIA'S SUPREME COURT: TRANSGENDER IS A THIRD LEGAL GENDER[8]

NEW DELHI—India's Supreme Court for the first time recognized a third gender Tuesday in a judgment aimed at giving transgender Indians their own legal status and better legal protection and privileges.

A two-judge bench ruled that transgender people will now have the option to identify themselves as a third gender—instead of just male or female—in government documents, including passports and identification cards.

The Supreme Court said discrimination based on gender identity or sexual orientation violates constitutional guarantees of equality, privacy and dignity.

"This is an extremely liberal and progressive decision that takes into consideration the ground realities for transgender people in India," said Anitha Shenoy, a lawyer who helped argue the case. "The court says your identity will be based not on your biology but on what you choose to be."

India is the latest of several South Asian countries to recognize a third gender. Neighboring Nepal has added a third gender option to government documents, as have Pakistan and Bangladesh. Germany became the first European country to recognize a third gender last year, allowing parents to mark "indeterminate" on birth certificates.

India's top court Tuesday also directed the federal and state governments to include transgender people as members of the

---

[8] Nikita Lalwani, The Wall Street Journal, April 15, 2014.

country's "backward classes," an official designation, often based on caste, which entitles socially and economically disadvantaged groups to affirmative action in school admissions and state employment.

The decision is revolutionary, some activists said, especially for a court that just last December reaffirmed a colonial-era law criminalizing homosexuality.

In that ruling, the court upheld Section 377 of the Indian penal code, which makes consensual gay sex punishable by a prison term of up to 10 years.

Tuesday's judgment pointed to the country's history of discrimination against transgender people. India's roughly three million transgender people are particularly vulnerable to public harassment, violence and sexual assault, the court said.

India has a vast and varied transgender community. Perhaps most prominent are the hijras, typically male to female transgender people who often live in close-knit groups and whose members are sometimes castrated.

Hijras have had a place in Indian society for centuries, and their presence at a wedding or after the birth of a child is considered auspicious. Still, they remain deeply marginalized.

In recognition of this deep-seated stigma, the court directed federal and state governments to address the "fear, shame, gender dysphoria, social pressure" and depression that afflict India's transgender community. It also said transgender people should have access to separate public toilet facilities.

Simran Shaikh, 31, an HIV/AIDS activist who identifies as hijra, said her gender expression has often triggered abuse. She doesn't use public transportation for fear of harassment and has been turned away from job interviews because of how she dresses.

"Until now, I had no legal rights and no legal identity," she said. "This wonderful verdict means I don't have to be a 'Mr.' or a 'Mrs.' I can just be Simran."

The verdict will create more education and employment opportunities for transgender people, said Abhina Aher, 37, who also identifies as hijra. She said she hopes it will also increase awareness of health issues, like HIV, prevalent in transgender communities.

With Tuesday's decision, India's top court appeared to return to its activist roots, said lawyer Menaka Guruswamy.

"The court is going back to what it has traditionally done, which is to expand rights, address disadvantages, and proscribe discrimination," Ms. Guruswamy said. "It's a tremendous ruling."

Although the judgment doesn't contest the validity of the December ruling banning gay sex, it acknowledges that Section 377 has been used historically as "an instrument of harassment and physical abuse" against transgender people.

"One bench clearly believes the statute has been used to harass and blackmail sexual minorities, while the other bench appears to ignore such harassment," Ms. Guruswamy said.

Activists are hopeful the Supreme Court will now revisit its December decision.

Anjali Gopalan, director of the Naz Foundation (India) Trust, the New Delhi-based NGO that filed a lawsuit challenging Section 377, called Tuesday's decision cause for optimism.

Tuesday's decision could also encourage the next government to repeal the colonial-era law, said Shailesh Rai, policy adviser at Amnesty International India.

9. INDIA COURT RECOGNISES TRANSGENDER PEOPLE AS 'THIRD GENDER'[9]

Transgender people in India have welcomed a landmark Supreme Court ruling that said all official documents must include the option for people to identify themselves as a third gender, for the first time offering a guarantee of human rights to around three million people.

The court ruled that the government must provide transgender people with equal access to education, healthcare and welfare programmes, and ordered a public awareness campaign be set up to tackle the stigma they face in day-to-day life.

Previously, India's transgender population has been ostracized and excluded from mainstream society because of their lack of legal recognition. Discriminated against and abused, many are forced into organised begging syndicates or prostitution.

Handing down the ruling yesterday, the Supreme Court declared it the right of every human being to choose their own gender. The new category defines anyone who does not identify with the gender on their birth certificate.

Lawyers said the decision means the government will have to allocate a certain percentage of all public sector jobs, seats in schools and colleges to transgender applicants, and separate facilities will have to be installed in all public toilets.

"Recognition of transgender [people] as a third gender is

[9] Adam Withnall, The Independent, April 16, 2014.

not a social or medical issue but a human rights issue," Justice KS Radhakrishnan told the court.

"Transgender [people] are also citizens of India", he said. "The spirit of the constitution is to provide equal opportunity to every citizen to grow and attain their potential, irrespective of caste, religion or gender."

Laxmi Narayan Tripathi, a transgender activist who petitioned the court alongside a legal agency, said: "Today I am proud to be an Indian."

"All documents will now have a third category marked 'transgender'. This verdict has come as a great relief for all of us.

Activists said the ruling was also an important step towards combatting hate crimes carried out against transgender people in the largely conservative country. Such incidents are common, they said, yet are rarely reported due to a perceived lack of interest or action from the police and other authorities.

The court also ruled that transgender people would have the same right to adopt children as other Indians, and that health departments must be created to take care of their medical problems.

Recently, India's Election Commission for the first time allowed a third gender choice — designated as "other" — on voter registration forms. The change was made in time for the national elections being held in phases through to 12 May, yet only 28,000 voters from a transgender population of millions registered themselves in that category.

The Supreme Court specified its ruling would only apply to transgender people and not to gay, lesbian or bisexual people.

It was criticized by human rights activists in December when it reinstated a colonial-era ban on gay sex, following a four-year period of decriminalization that helped bring homosexuality into the open. The court said only parliament could change the law.

Activists said they hoped the ruling on transgender people would encourage the new parliament to repeal the anti-homosexuality law as one of its first actions after the election results are released on 16 May.

10. INDIA'S SUPREME COURT CREATES OFFICIAL THIRD SEX FOR EUNUCHS AND TRANSGENDERS[10]

India's Supreme Court has created an official third sex for its transgender eunuchs and announced they will have a quota of government jobs and college places to help them overcome discrimination.

The decision was met with jubilation by transgender charities who said it was a milestone in their fight against marginalisation in Indian society.

"We are elated and thankful to the court," said Kalki Subramanium, a leading transgender rights activist. "The decision has come after a century of suppression and marginalisation by the legal and social systems.

"This verdict is certainly landmark and a new beginning. The biggest challenge is the social recognition. We have to educate and make people aware that we exist and there's nothing abnormal about us. This will give a boost to the transgenders who want to study or work but were denied a chance. They can now be part of the mainstream,"

India's transgenders include those who feel they were born into the wrong sex, men born with deformed genitals and effeminate boys disowned by their families and sent to live in eunuch colonies.

---

[10] Dean Nelson, The Telegraph, 15 April 2014.

The court ruled that those who have been castrated or undergone gender reassignment surgery, as well as those who present themselves as not of the sex they were born into, can all be classified as transgender.

There are just under two million eunuchs and transgenders in India, many of whom live in groups controlled by a eunuch guru and survive by aggressive begging. Although marginalised, they are widely feared. They often turn up at weddings and after the birth of boys to demand large donations for their blessings. Many pay in fear of their curse or embarrassment – they often hitch up their saris and reveal their mutilated genitalia outside the homes of those who refuse.

In the capital New Delhi some eunuchs operate as organised extortion gangs and their "tolly" collections are so successful there have been calls for them to be hired as tax collectors to boost revenues.

Their fortunes in India have varied throughout the ages. They are mentioned derisively in the Hindu epic, the Mahabharata, but were influential in the royal household during the Mughal period when they were trusted as courtiers and harem guards.

Today many of those living in eunuch communities have been rejected by their families either because they were born with deformed genitalia or were effeminate. Some of them have undergone distressing and dangerous village castrations to become hijras.

In its ruling, the Supreme Court said the Indian constitution provides equal opportunity "irrespective of caste, religion or gender". Justice K.S. Radhakrishnan said the "recognition of transgender (people) as a third gender is not a social or medical issue but a human rights issue."

It ordered the government to launch public awareness campaigns to end the stigma transgenders suffer.

Transgender campaigners hope the decision and their acceptance for government quotas will mean more fulfilling career opportunities in the future. A number of eunuchs have won elections in India – one was elected mayor in Sagar, Madhya Pradesh, in 2009 - and some have had some success in film and television.

Few, if any, have succeeded in mainstream professions.

11. SUPREME COURT RECOGNISES TRANSGENDER PEOPLE AS A "THIRD GENDER" AS IT CALLS FOR AN END TO DISCRIMINATION[11]

In a historic judgment that will pave the way for lakhs of transgender people to join the mainstream, the Supreme Court on Tuesday granted legal recognition to the community as a third gender.

Upholding their demand for equal treatment with males and females, the court directed the Central and state governments to treat transgender people as "socially and educationally backward classes" and to give them reservation in educational institutions and for appointment in PSUs.

Significantly, the court also said that if a person surgically changes his or her sex, then the person is entitled to the changed sex and cannot be discriminated against, as widely happens.

"By recognising transgender as third gender, this court is not only upholding the rule of law but also advancing justice to the class, so far deprived of their legitimate natural and constitutional rights," said a bench of Justices K.S. Radhakrishnan and A.K. Sikri.

Authorities were directed to take steps to remove several problems faced by the community such as fear, shame, depression, and social stigma.

---

[11] Harish V. Nair, Mail Online India, 15 April 2014.

Acceptance

However, the bench clarified its verdict pertained only to eunuchs and not to gays, lesbians and bisexuals.

The verdict came in response to a PIL filed by the National Legal Services Authority (NALSA), which brought to the court's attention the discrimination faced by the community.

Welcoming the verdict, Asha Menon, member secretary of NALSA, said: "It would result in confidence building in the community and compel the society to look towards this section of people with acceptance."

The bench said: "Discrimination faced by this group in our society is rather unimaginable and their rights have to be protected, irrespective of chromosomal sex, genitals, assigned birth sex, or implied gender role."

Expressing concern over transgender people being harassed and discriminated against, the court said the community was earlier respected in society but now, for no reason, they are perceived to be persons who indulge in child kidnapping and unnatural offences.

Non-recognition of the identity of 'hijras' or transgender people denies them equal protection of law, thereby leaving them extremely vulnerable to harassment and sexual assault in public spaces, at home and in jail, as well as by the police.

Sexual assault, including molestation, rape, forced anal and oral sex and stripping is being committed with impunity, and there are reliable statistics and materials to support this, it said.

Transgender people were included as a separate category in the national census for the first time in 2011.

Two years ago, the Election Commission allowed them to be registered under the "other" category on voters' rolls, since which time over 28,000 transgender people have been registered by the poll panel.

Pakistan and Nepal beat India to it

In September 2012, Pakistan's SC ruled that transgender people have the same rights as other citizens in matters of inheritance, education and employment.

The court ordered authorities in November 2011 to register transgender people as voters and issue them National ID Cards with a gender of their choice.

As per official records, there are 80,000 transgender people in Pakistan. In December 2007, Nepal's SC declared full and fundamental human rights for all "sexual and gender minorities".

The court ordered the government to scrap all discriminatory laws and legally established a "third gender" category.

In January 2013, Nepal officially included the third gender on citizenship certificates and other documents.

12. INDIA NOW RECOGNIZES TRANSGENDER CITIZENS AS 'THIRD GENDER'[12]

In India, as in almost every nation in the West, members of the transgender population have historically been forced to designate themselves as either a "male" or "female" on all governmental forms.

No Longer

In what local media are calling a landmark judgment, India's Supreme Court on Tuesday created a "third gender" status for transgender people, granting the group formal recognition for the first time. "Recognition of transgenders as a third gender is not a social or medical issue but a human rights issue," Justice K.S. Radhakrishnan said when he announced the ruling. "Transgenders are citizens of this country and are entitled to education and all other rights."

He directed local governmental bureaucracies to identify transgender people as a neutral third gender, adding that they will now have the same access to social welfare programs as other minority groups in India, the world's largest democracy and currently in the midst an election campaign.

The court's decision would apply to individuals who have acquired the physical characteristics of the opposite sex or present

---

[12] Terrence McCoy, The Washington Post, April 15, 2014.

themselves in a way that does not correspond with their sex at birth, the Associated Press said.

The Supreme Court specified that its ruling would apply only to transgender people and not to gays, lesbians or bisexuals. India's LGBT communities have been protesting the court's recent decision to reinstate a colonial-era law banning gay sex, which they say will make them vulnerable to police harassment.

The case was brought in 2012 when a group led by transgender activist Laxmi Narayan Tripathi, a Hindi film actress, sought equal rights for India's transgender population.

On Tuesday, Tripathi was triumphant. "Today, for the first time I feel very proud to be an Indian," she told reporters gathered at the New Delhi court. "Today, my sisters and I feel like real Indians, and we feel so proud because of the rights granted to us by the Supreme Court."

Across much of South Asia and Southeast Asia, the language of gender is substantially more ambiguous than it is in the West. In countries such as Thailand and Cambodia, transgender people aren't usually referred to as either a man or a woman — but as *kathoey*. India's decision follows other regional countries' decisions to recognize a third gender. Last year, neighboring Nepal offered a third gender option on official documents for its transgender population.

The West has been a tad slower to adopt such measures. Last year, Germany became the first European country to recognize a third gender, allowing parents of newborns to mark "male," "female" or "indeterminate" on birth certificates.

Across the rest of Europe, Spiegel Online reports, change has been more halting. "Things are moving slower than they should at the European level," human rights activist Silvan Agius said. "Though Brussels has ramped up efforts to promote awareness of trans and intersex discrimination, I would like to see things speed up."

Things in India sped up this year. For the first time, India's Election Commission allowed a third gender of "other" on voter registration forms for this election. Nearly 30,000 people designated themselves as "other," the Associated Press reported, and there are an estimated 3 million transgender individuals in India.

"The progress of the country is dependent upon [the] human rights of the people, and we are very happy with the judgment," Tripathi said. "The Supreme Court has given us those rights.